# Glen R Stansfield

The Man in a Hat

7 St John Street, Creetown, Newton Stewart DG8 7JA

Copyright © 2018 Glen R Stansfield

Glen R Stansfield has asserted his right to be identified as the author of this work.

British spelling is used throughout.

All rights reserved. No part of this publication may be reproduced, stored in a retrieval system, or transmitted, in any form or by any means, without the prior permission in writing of the Publisher, or as expressly permitted by law, by licence or under terms agreed with the appropriate reprographics rights organisation. Enquiries concerning reproduction outside the scope of the above should be sent to the Publisher, at the address above.

This book is sold subject to the condition that it shall not, by way of trade or otherwise, be lent, resold, hired out, or otherwise circulated without the publisher's prior consent in any form of binding or cover other than that with which it is published and without similar condition, including this condition being imposed on the subsequent purchaser.

ISBN: 9781912378067

Printed by Lightning Source,
Great Britain, United States and Australia

# Around the World in Eighty Dishes

**To my wife Jess, who had to put up with the messy kitchen.**

# Around the World in Eighty Dishes

# Acknowledgements

These are the people that in one way or another made this book possible. My thanks go to the following, and I hope I have not forgotten anyone;

Sue Noyes for her proofreading and editing - https://suenoyes.com

Jo at BCB for his excellent work on the cover - http://bookcover.biz

Mehr Jan of Weekender, for her continuous encouragement and support while writing the series.

The many chefs and cooks around the world, who produce some incredible dishes from the simplest ingredients.

And not least my wife Jess, who had to put up with the weekly buying of ingredients, photography, preparation, cooking, more photography and finally eating whatever concoction I made that week, as well as cleaning the inevitable disaster area of a kitchen.

All photographs © **Glen R Stansfield** except the following;
Weekender logo, cover © **Weekender**
Around the World in Eighty Dishes logo, title and half title pages © **Weekender**
World Map, Page 2 © **ekler/Shutterstock**
Spices, page 11 © **Monticello/Shutterstock**

# Around the World in Eighty Dishes

The journey we are undertaking finds its roots far earlier than my childhood when I helped my mother to bake. In fact, we need to go back to 1873 when something occurred that would influence me as a child and throughout my adulthood.

It took almost 100 years for there to be any effect on my life, but that happened when as a child, I was allowed to borrow some books from the adult section of the library. The first was 'Around the World in Eighty Days.'

The author, Jules Verne, was a great visionary in his writing, with prophecies of going to the moon, and travelling vast distances under the sea. But it was the journey of Phileas Fogg that first captured my imagination, inspired me to write, and gave me a yearning to travel which is still with me to this day.

I am not a professional cook or chef, I am an aircraft engineer by trade, as well as an author of fiction. From an early age, I had an interest in the preparation and consumption of food (particularly the consumption!), often helping my mother bake. As I grew older, I tried making my own variations of recipes, sometimes with disastrous results, but on occasion something edible emerged.

So, it seemed the most obvious thing to do would be to combine my love of food with my desire to travel and embark upon a journey of discovery of the foods and people of the world.

In case you are wondering why we are not following the original route of Phileas Fogg, much of his journey was at sea, not the ideal place to find creative recipes. Why did we not start and finish at the Reform Club? These recipes first appeared as a weekly feature in Weekender, a Bahrain publication, and started in the Holy month of Ramadan 2016. Mehr Jan, the editor of Weekender, thought it would be fitting to start the journey in Mecca, the centre of Islam, and so it was. Although we do not return to Mecca for the final dish, we have circumnavigated the world. All recipes are halal and have been adapted where necessary to make them so.

I cooked and photographed each recipe, then both my wife and I ate the results, and we are still here to tell the tale. Don't be afraid to try something new, and as with all cooking, experiment, have fun, and be creative.

## Welcome to my,

## 'Around the World in Eighty Dishes.'

**Glen R Stansfield.**
**Author, biker and nutcase**
**Bahrain, 2018**

# Around the World in Eighty Dishes

# Contents

      2 Map
   4-11 Middle East
 12-15 North Africa
 16-27 Central Africa
 28-37 Southern Africa
 38-69 Asia/Far East
 70-81 Australasia
 82-89 Pacific
 90-107 South America
110-121 Central America
122-131 North America
132-163 Europe
   164 Conversion tables
   166 Index

# Around the World in Eighty Dishes

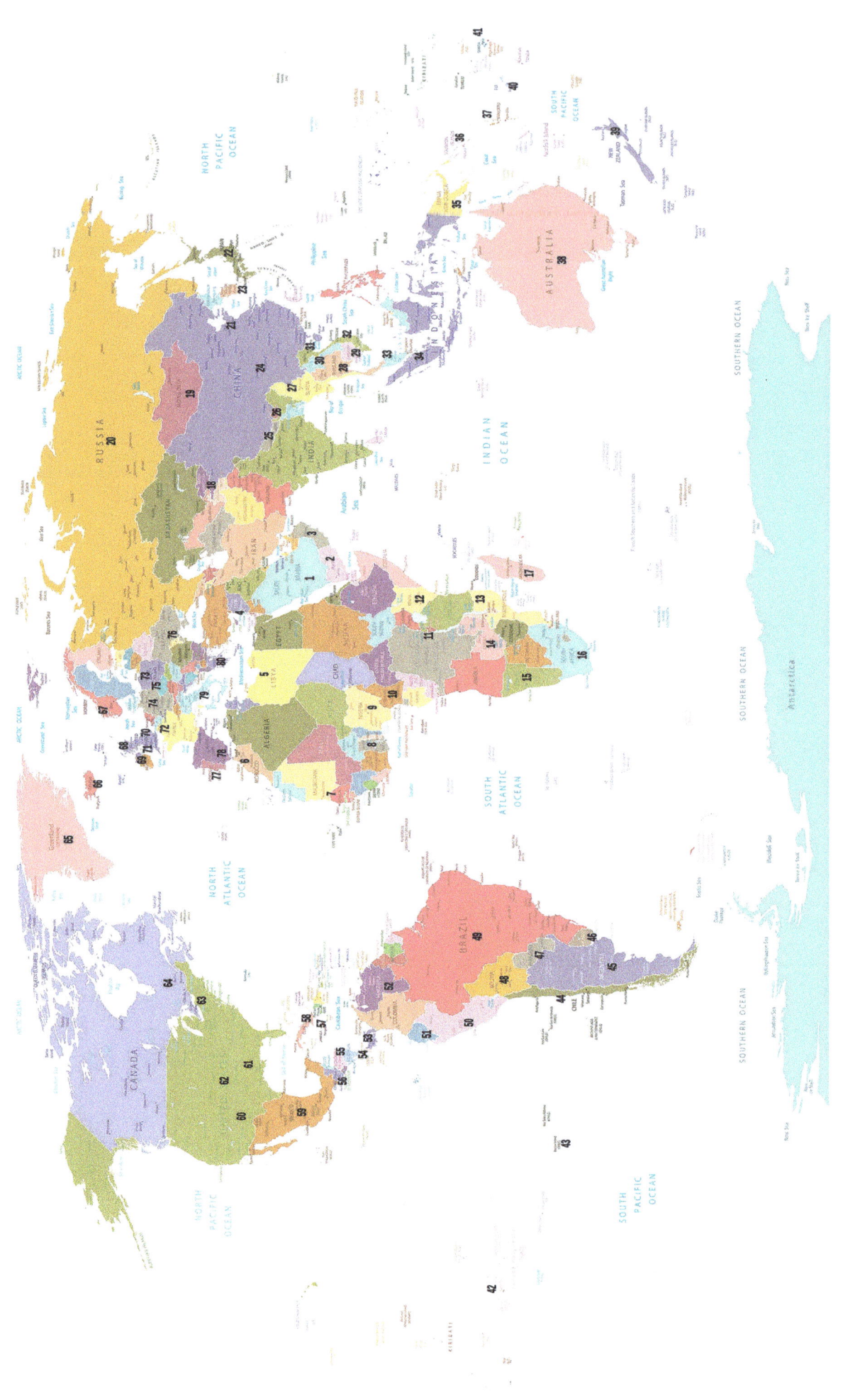

# Around the World in Eighty Dishes

## Key to map

1 **Saudi Arabia** - Fish Kabsa
2 **Yemen** - Mutabbaq
3 **Oman** - Halawah
4 **Lebanon** - Chicken and Potatoes
5 **Libya** - Mb'atten
6 **Morocco** -.Harira
7 **Gambia/Senegal** - Chicken Yassa
8 **Ghana** - West African Peanut Soup
9 **Nigeria** - Puff Puff
10 **Cameroon** - Suya and Jelouf Rice
11 **Burundi** - Banana and Date Mix
12 **Kenya** - Kuku Wa Kupaka
13 **Mozambique** - Bolo Polana
14 **Zambia** - Curried Gazelle
15 **Namibia** - Ginger and Quince Stew
16 **South Africa** – Bobotie
17 **Madagascar** - Veal Chops in Green Peppercorn Sauce
18 **Kyrgyzstan** - Laghman
19 **Mongolia** - Khuushuur
20 **Russia** - Black Bread
21 **China** - Shandong Chicken
22 **Japan** - Tempura
23 **Korea** - Fried Fish. Rice with Mushrooms
24 **China** - Sichuan Stir-Fry
25 **Nepal** - Aloo Dam
26 **Bhutan** - Ema Datshi
27 **Myanmar** - Beya Kya
28 **Thailand** - Thai Green Curry
29 **Cambodia** - Amok Trei
30 **Laos** - Tam Som Salad
31 **Vietnam** - Pho Bo
32 **Vietnam** - Banh Mi
33 **Malaysia** - Curry Puffs
34 **Indonesia** - Beef Rendang
35 **Papua New Guinea** - Banana Pancakes
36 **Solomon Islands** - Tuna and Noodles
37 **Vanuatu** - Mango Chutney
38 **Australia** - Macadamia Nut Cookies
39 **New Zealand** - Sweet & Sour Beef
40 **Fiji** - Sweet Potato and Pineapple Bake
41 **Samoa** - Sapa Sui
42 **Tahiti** - Tahitian Marinated Fresh Fish
43 **Easter Island** - Po'e

44 **Chile** - Cazuela de Vaca
45 **Argentina** - Spicy Bread
46 **Uruguay** - El Postre Chaja
47 **Paraguay** - Vori Vori de Pollo
48 **Bolivia** - Silpacho
49 **Brazil** - Vatapá
50 **Peru** - Papas Rellenas
51 **Ecuador** - Pescado a la Parrilla con Salsa de Mariscos
52 **Venezuela** - Tequenos con Guasacaca
53 **Panama** - Salpicón de Res (beef salad shredded)
54 **Costa Rica** - Casado
55 **Nicaragua** - Berenjenas Rellenas
56 **Guatemala** - Carne en Jocon
57 **Jamaica** - Goat Curry
58 **Cuba** - Cangrejos Enchilados
59 **Mexico** - Huevos Rancheros
60 **USA** - Fajitas
61 **USA** - Gumbo
62 **USA** - Fried Rabbit with Corn Blueberry and Wild Rice Salad
63 **USA** - Apple Pie
64 **Canada** - Venison with Sweet Potato Dauphinoise
65 **Greenland** - Summer Casserole
66 **Iceland** - Lamb Soup (kjotsupa)
67 **Norway** -Smoked Salmon and Scrambled Egg
68 **Scotland** - Clootie Dumpling
69 **Ireland** - Colcannon
70 **England** - Banoffee Pie
71 **Wales** - Mountain Lamb with Honey and Herbs
72 **France** - Crème Caramel
73 **Poland** - Blueberry Pierogi
74 **Germany** - Beef Short Ribs Sauerbraten
75 **Czech Republic** - Langoš
76 **Ukraine** - Borscht
77 **Portugal** - Bacalhau à Bras
78 **Spain** - Paella
79 **Italy** - Ravioli Fois Gras
80 **Greece** - Saganaki Garides

# 1 - Fish Kabsa - Saudi Arabia

At one time, the peoples of the Makkah Region, around the Holy City of Mecca would have used mainly meat in their dishes, particularly lamb and chicken. As trade developed with the people of the coastal regions, fish featured more widely in their diets and recipes were adapted to reflect this.

The origin of this dish is somewhat blurred, as is the case with many of the recipes from the Middle East. As nomads moved from place to place, so did their ways of cooking. The tribes and the regions would discover new methods and ingredients, resulting in many variations of the same dish.

Although Kabsa can be found throughout the Middle East, where it is also known as Makbus, it is widely regarded as a national dish of Saudi Arabia.

## What you need

4 tbs butter
6 garlic cloves, finely chopped
1 white onion, finely chopped
½ tbs kabsa spice mix (see below)
1 kg white fish fillet cut into large pieces
1 vegetable stock cube or stock pot
2 tbs tomato paste
390 g basmati rice
1 litre water
sea salt and freshly ground black pepper
35 g pine nuts
handful chopped coriander

## What to do

Use a large pan over a medium heat, add the onion, garlic and butter. Cook until the onion is tender. Add the Kabsa mix and stir well. Lower the pieces of fish gently into the pan and cook on both sides until the fish is white. Remove the fish from the pan and set aside.

Add the stock cube, tomato paste, rice and water to the pan. Increase the heat until the water is boiling then cover the pan and turn the heat to low. Cook for 20 minutes.

While the rice mixture is cooking, toast the pine nuts in a dry frying pan until lightly browned.

When the rice is cooked, return the fish to the pan on top of the rice and allow to heat through for 5 minutes. Season to taste.

Arrange on a serving platter and sprinkle with the toasted pine nuts and chopped coriander.
Serve with a fresh salad.

## Cook's tip:

Kabsa mix can be purchased ready made from many supermarkets and spice merchants, or you can make your own as follows;

## What you need

1 tsp turmeric (or 23 strands of saffron)
1 tsp coriander seed
1 tsp black pepper corns
1 tsp cardamom seed
1 tsp ginger (ground)
1 tsp fennel seed
1 tsp cumin seed

# 1 - Fish Kabsa - Saudi Arabia

**What to do**

Grind the ingredients together using a mortar and pestle or use a coffee/spice grinder if you wish to give your muscles a rest. Store the mix in an airtight jar in a cool dark place.

# 2 - Mutabbaq - Yemen

Of the many things written about mutabbaq, the one thing that most agree on is the dish probably originated in Yemen. Indian traders took the recipe back to their home country and from there it spread to South East Asia. There are a few that say the dish originated in India and spread out from there along the trade routes. Whichever it is, there is no doubting it is a satisfying snack, or even a main meal if you wish.

Mutabbaq, fatatari, murtabak or martabak as it is known in the different regions, can be made with many variations of the ingredients.

## What you need

### For the dough*

260 g all-purpose flour
1 tsp salt
milk as required

*As an alternative, spring roll wrappers may be used

### For the filling

ghee or butter for shallow frying
20 garlic cloves, finely chopped
5-10 green chillies, finely chopped
2 onions, finely chopped
250 g minced lamb, or mutton
generous handful coriander and mint leaves, finely chopped
1 tsp salt
½ tsp black pepper
1 tsp allspice powder
3 eggs
handful finely chopped green part of spring onion (leek can be used instead)
3 tomatoes, chopped

## What to do

Add salt to the flour and sift into a mixing bowl.

Add a small quantity milk as required and knead until a smooth dough is formed. Divide according to the size of mutabbaq you wish to make. In this example, the mutabbaq was served as a main meal and so was divided into larger portions.

Add 2 tbs of ghee to a large heavy based frying pan and gently fry the garlic, chillies and onions until the onions are clear. Add the mince, coriander, mint, salt, pepper and allspice powder and fry until the meat is cooked and any water is removed. Remove from the heat and allow to cool for at least 15 minutes.

Roll out the dough on a smooth oiled surface until almost see through. Add the eggs, spring onion and chopped tomato to the mince in the pan and mix together. Spoon a portion of the mixture into the dough and fold over the sides to form a square parcel. Heat some ghee in a second frying pan and fry the parcel on a medium heat until golden on both sides. Keep in a warm oven until all parcels are cooked.

Don't be afraid to try other spices and ingredients to vary the filling.

# 2 - Mutabbaq - Yemen

**Cook's tip:**

To save time, add all the ingredients for the filling together (except the onion) in an electric chopper, chop them finely then fry them all together with the hand chopped onion, before adding the mince. (Chopping onion in an electric machine can cause it to taste bitter).

# 3 - Halawah - Oman

Halawah or halwa, meaning 'sweet,' is a generic name for many dishes throughout the world. You are no doubt familiar with some of the varieties yourself. The texture of the dish varies widely, from jelly like, to crumbly, depending on the ingredients. Whatever they are made from all of them have one thing in common, they are incredibly sweet and certainly not for the calorie conscious!

In Oman, this dish is made from dates and sugar, thickened with tapioca and flavoured with rosewater. It is something of a cottage industry with families keeping their recipes a closely guarded secret; passing them down from generation to generation. No self-respecting Omani dessert table would be without at least one version of this sweet and tasty dish.

## What you need

500 g dates, pitted and finely chopped
750 ml water
100 g sugar
3 tbs tapioca, dissolved in 60 ml water
50 g slivered and toasted almonds
50 g butter
2 tsp rosewater
1/4 tsp ground cardamom seeds
1/4 tsp ground nutmeg

## What to do

Bring the dates and water to the boil in a saucepan, stir frequently. Continue to cook over medium/low heat for 1 minute while stirring, adding more water if required. Add the sugar and cook for a few minutes (see note below) then stir in the dissolved tapioca. Cook over low heat until the mixture thickens, stirring continuously. Add the remaining ingredients (the nuts can be chopped and added now or reserved for decoration), and cook for 2 minutes, stirring continually. Allow to cool for a few hours in a refrigerator. Decorate with the nuts if not previously stirred into the mixture.

## Cook's tip:

If necessary, pass the mixture through a sieve to remove any part of the dates which didn't dissolve in cooking. Return to the pan before adding the tapioca mix.

# 3 - Halawah - Oman

# 4 - Chicken and Potatoes - Lebanon

As a country in its own right, Lebanon is relatively young, only coming into existence under French control as the state of Greater Lebanon in 1920. From the 16th century, the region had been part of the Ottoman Empire. Lebanon as we know it today gained its independence in 1943. But a political state and the people are not the same thing, and the earliest evidence of civilisation in the area dates back to 5,000 BC.

As we see with recipes from other countries in the Middle East, merchants who travelled the trade routes brought with them new methods of cooking and spices from distant lands. The Ottoman Turks introduced a variety of foods many of which have become a staple part of the Lebanese diet. Olive oil, fresh bread, baklava, laban and stuffed vegetables, to name but a few. The French also had an influence, with croissants and caramel custard becoming firm favourites.

It is easy to see why, with such diverse influences, Lebanese cooking is some of the most popular in the Middle East

## What you need

2 chicken pieces
5 medium potatoes
4 tbs olive oil
pinch Lebanese 7 spice (See below)
Salt
2 lemons, juiced
15-20 cloves garlic
(less if you don't like too much garlic)

## What to do

Make cuts in the chicken then place in the bottom of a roasting tin or dish. Rub with 1 tbs of olive oil. Sprinkle with a pinch of Lebanese 7 spice and salt to taste.

Wash and peel the potatoes then slice about 1 cm thick. Cover the chicken with the potatoes and lightly salt.

Bake at 200°C for 40-50 minutes or until the chicken is cooked through.

While the chicken is cooking, place the garlic and 3 tbs of olive oil in a blender and blend until smooth. Add the lemon juice and continue blending until the sauce is well mixed.

Once the chicken is cooked, drain any juices from the pan then pour the garlic sauce over the potatoes, mixing well.

Grill for 5-10 minutes until the potatoes start to turn golden brown.

Serve hot.

# 4 - Chicken and Potatoes - Lebanon

**To make Lebanese 7 spice mix**

Mix together the following
1 tsp ground nutmeg
1 tsp ground ginger
1 tsp ground allspice
1 tsp ground fenugreek
1 tsp ground cloves
1 tsp ground cinnamon
1 tsp ground black pepper

Store in an airtight jar in a cool dry place.

# 5 - Mb'atten - Libya

Potatoes are native to South America and did not reach Europe until the 16th century when they were brought back by the Spanish Conquistadores, but it wasn't until the 18th century they started to gain popularity. The history of the potato in Africa is a little less clear, but it is thought that they were introduced by colonists from the late 16th century onwards. Exactly when the potato arrived in Libya is not documented but it is thought to have been established well before the arrival of the Italians in the early part of the 20th century.

Libyan food has been influenced by many cultures, resulting in an interesting fusion of Arab, Mediterranean and African foods and methods. Grains were the most prominent feature of the Libyan diet in the days of the Romans, whilst in the 8th century the Arabs brought spices from as far away as India and China. With the invasion of the Turks and the time of the Ottoman Empire came a new method of preparation in the form of barbecuing, and lastly the Italians brought pasta. Although mb'atten is considered to be a traditional dish and is thought to be unique to Libya, its origins have been lost in time.

## What you need

500 g minced lamb (or beef)
3 green chillies, finely chopped
¼ tsp cinnamon powder
1 tsp paprika
½ tsp of turmeric powder
2 tomatoes finely chopped
3 garlic cloves, finely chopped
1 onion, finely chopped
handful finely chopped parsley
handful finely chopped dill
6 spring onions, only the white part, chopped,
salt
2 eggs
3-4 large white potatoes
flour
vegetable oil for frying

## What to do

Mix together the chilli, cinnamon, paprika, turmeric, tomatoes, garlic, onion, parsley, dill and spring onions with the meat. Beat one egg and add to the mixture, combine well and season.

Peel the potatoes, then starting about 3 mm from one end, slice roughly ¾ of the way through **(Fig 1),** then make the next cut all the way down the potato **(Fig 2).** You should be left with a slice of potato around 6 mm thick with a pocket in the centre **(Fig 3)**. Make as many as you need to use all the filling.

# 5 - Mb'atten - Libya

Take a potato pocket and fill it with the meat mixture, then dip the open end in the beaten egg and then the flour. This is to stop the mixture falling out when frying.
When all the slices are prepared, cook in batches as follows;
Heat the oil to 120°C and lower the slices into the oil. Cook for approximately 3 minutes then remove and drain. When all the slices are done, heat the oil to 180°C.
Return the slices to the oil and cook until golden and crisp.
Place the fried mb'atten on kitchen paper to drain excess oil then sprinkle with salt.
Serve immediately.

Fig 1　　　　　　　　Fig 2　　　　　　　　Fig 3

# 6 - Harira - Morocco

There are almost as many recipes for Harira as there are stars in the sky, and it isn't surprising. Moroccan food has been influenced by Arabic, African, French, Mediterranean and Middle Eastern cooking, as the merchants from these regions followed the trade routes to and from Morocco.

Traditionally served for Iftar during Ramadan, this delicious soup can also be a snack or a main meal at any time of the year.

Harira is a tomato-based soup with lamb, chickpeas, lentils and pasta, infused with the flavours of cinnamon, coriander, parsley, turmeric, and ginger, and thickened with flour. Serve with crusty bread and a segment of lemon, which should be squeezed into the soup to personal taste. An additional bowl of lemon juice can be provided for those who like the extra tang.

Variations in the recipes can include; chicken with the lamb, rice instead of pasta and thickening with egg. Most families in Morocco will have their favourite recipe and ingredients.

## What you need

450-600 g lamb cut into 1 cm cubes
1 tsp ground cinnamon
¼ tsp ground ginger
¼ tsp ground cayenne pepper or paprika
1½ tsp ground black pepper
1 tsp ground turmeric
2 tbs butter
2 sticks celery
2 onions, chopped
handful chopped fresh coriander
handful chopped fresh parsley
500 g tomatoes, chopped
2.3 litres water, or lamb stock
4 tbs tomato puree
200 g green lentils
100 g long-grain rice
400 g can chickpeas, drained or dried chickpeas, soaked overnight
2 eggs, beaten
1 lemon, segmented

## What to do

Place a large saucepan on a medium heat. Add the lamb, cinnamon, ginger, paprika, pepper, turmeric, butter celery, onions, fresh coriander and parsley. Cook for 5 minutes, stirring frequently. Add the tomatoes and cook for a further 15 minutes, continuing to stir. Add the water, lentils and tomato puree, stir well then reduce to a gentle simmer. Cover and cook for 1½ hours.

Add the rice and cook for a further 30 minutes. Remove from the heat and add the chickpeas, allowing them to warm through, then slowly stir in the beaten egg. Allow the egg to cook for a few minutes before serving with a segment of lemon.

## Cook's tip:

If using pasta instead of rice, add the pasta after 1 hour 50 minutes of cooking, and cook for a further 10 minutes, before adding the chickpeas and egg.

To thicken with flour instead of egg: slowly add 300 ml of water to 1 heaped tbs of all-purpose flour and mix into a smooth cream. Add to the pan at the end of cooking and bring back to the simmer before serving.

# 6 - Harira - Morocco

# 7 - Chicken Yassa - Gambia/Senegal

The ethnic mix of Senegal is quite diverse, each bringing their own traditions, ingredients and methods of cooking. This area has been populated for thousands of years and as result, Senegalese cuisine is influenced by many other parts of Africa, particularly the North, but has seen influences from much further afield. As we see with many of the countries we visit, European traders, particularly French, Portuguese, Dutch and English, all brought their own ingredients and cooking styles with them.

Initially, the primary trade was slaves, although this eventually gave way to commodity trading, especially acacia gum and peanuts.

## What you need

1 chicken, cut into serving sized pieces
4-6 onions, thinly sliced
8 tbs lime juice
8 tbs cider vinegar
1 bay leaf
4 cloves finely chopped or minced garlic
1 tbs soy sauce or chicken stock
1 or 2 chillies finely chopped (or one Habanero, deseeded)
1 tsp cayenne pepper
2 tsp coarsely ground black pepper
1 carrot, thinly sliced
groundnut oil for frying
1 tsp whole allspice

## What to do

Mix together all the ingredients (except the carrot, allspice and oil), and place in a glass bowl or a large re-sealable bag. Add the chicken and cover the bowl (if using). Marinate in the refrigerator for a few hours or preferably overnight.

Remove chicken from the marinade, reserving the marinade. Sauté the chicken pieces for a few minutes on each side in hot oil in a large saucepan. Remove and set aside. Add the allspice to the pan and cook for about 2 minutes until fragrant.

Strain the marinade, reserving the liquid, then add the solids to the saucepan. Sauté for a few minutes until the onions start to soften. Add reserved liquid and the sliced carrot then bring to a slow boil, cooking the marinade into a sauce. Add chicken to the sauce, reduce the heat. Cover the pan then simmer until chicken is done. Remove the chicken and keep warm.

Continue to cook the onions until the liquid has evaporated and the onions start to caramelise.
Place the chicken on a bed of white rice or couscous and cover with the onions.

# 7 - Chicken Yassa - Gambia/Senegal

# 8 - West African Peanut Stew - Ghana

Peanuts, or groundnuts as they are also known, are not native to Africa. They were brought from South America by Spanish and Portuguese colonists in the latter part of the 16th century. This stew is popular in West Africa, especially Nigeria, the Gambia and Senegal.

A variety of ingredients can be used and vary by region, but can include root vegetables like yams, cooked greens, okra, squash, eggplant, beans and corn.

This particular version is from Ghana and uses a hot chilli, the Habanero. You can substitute something less spicy if you wish.

## What you need

1 whole chicken
3 tbs groundnut oil
1 large onion, sliced
large piece of ginger, peeled and minced
6-8 garlic cloves, roughly chopped
1 large sweet potato, peeled and cut into chunks
1 African yam
1 litre chicken stock
1 Habanero chilli, deseeded and finely chopped
4 tomatoes, roughly chopped
270 g peanut butter
140 g roasted peanuts
1 tbs ground coriander
1 tsp cayenne pepper
salt and black pepper
handful chopped coriander

## What to do

Quarter the chicken. Heat the oil in a large stock pan and brown the chicken pieces on both sides. Set aside once browned.

Sauté the onions for 3-4 minutes, stirring often and scraping off the bottom of the pan. Add the ginger and garlic and cook for a further 12 minutes then add the sweet potato and yam. Mix thoroughly. Add the chicken, stock, chilli, chopped tomatoes, peanut butter, peanuts, coriander and cayenne. Combine well. Bring to a simmer test for seasoning, adding salt as required. Cover and simmer gently for 90 minutes (check the pan after an hour), or until the chicken falls off the bone and the sweet potatoes and yam are tender.

Remove the chicken pieces and allow to cool. Remove and discard the skin or chop into small pieces to return to the pan. Shred the chicken from the bones and return to the pan.

Check for seasoning, then add black pepper to preference. The stew should be peppery to the taste. Garnish with the chopped coriander and serve with crusty bread or steamed rice.

## Cook's tip:

To make a good chicken stock, simmer chicken bones, chopped onion, chopped celery and chopped carrot in water for 2-3 hours. To make thicker, add chicken feet to the recipe. For stronger stock, replace the water with chicken stock you have already made.

## To make peanut butter

Roast 500 g raw, shelled and skinned peanuts for approximately 10 minutes. Place in a food blender with ½ tsp salt and blend for three minutes, drizzling in groundnut oil to make the mix

# 8 - West African Peanut Stew - Ghana

smoother. Using a rubber spatula, scrape the sides of the blender and return to the mix. Continue blending and scraping until creamy.

**Cook's tip:**

The mix will never be as smooth as shop bought peanut butter, but neither will it have other ingredients added unless you wish to do so. Store in a jar in the refrigerator for up to 2 months.

# 9 - Puff Puff - Nigeria

All over the world there are recipes that fry leavened and sweetened dough. These delicacies can have many names, the most common being doughnut or the more modern spelling, donut.
In Nigeria, the dish is known as Puff Puff where it isn't just another dish, it almost is an institution in its own right.
No self-respecting Nigerian hostess would organise a party without providing Puff Puff for her guests.
Visit Nigeria and you will find Puff Puff available from street vendors on almost every street corner.
This recipe is easy to make, and you will soon find this is one snack you cannot stop eating.

## What you need

½ tbs salt
470 ml warm water
1 packet active dry yeast
420 g all-purpose flour
125 g sugar
Oil for deep frying

## What to do

Mix salt, water, yeast and sugar. Stand for 5 minutes.
Add the flour and mix well.
Let the mixture rise for approximately 1-2 hours (it will double in size and contain lots of small bubbles).
Use either a deep fat fryer or a large pan (containing at least 8 cm of oil) and put on a low-medium heat.
Test the oil to make sure it is hot enough by putting a 'drop' of batter into the oil. If it is hot enough, the batter will rise to the top of the pan.
When the oil is hot enough, grab a little bit of the mixture in the palm of your hand, and squeeze out a ball of batter between your thumb and index finger (It takes practice but is really easy once you have the hang of it). Alternatively, use a spoon to dish up the batter, and another spoon or spatula to drop it in the oil, in the shape of a ball.
Drop the ball of batter carefully into the oil, taking care not to splash. Fry until the one side is golden brown, then turn the ball over and fry until the other side is the same.
Using a slotted spoon, remove the balls and place onto kitchen paper to drain.
Roll in granulated or icing sugar.

## Cook's tip:

If using a deep fat fryer, do not use the basket unless you want one large Puff Puff attached to a basket!
If you sprinkle the Puff Puff with icing sugar while hot, the sugar melts onto the Puff Puff and forms a rudimentary glaze.

## 9 - Puff Puff - Nigeria

# 10 - Suya and Jelouf Rice - Cameroon

Although we see the world as divided into countries, separated by borders which are sometimes vigorously defended, the people of the lands often exist cross-border. This is particularly evident with the Hausa Tribe, whose roots can be traced back to Stone Age times. One of the largest tribes of West Africa, the Hausa people can be found in northern Nigeria, south-eastern Niger, with significant populations in Chad, Côte d'Ivoire, Ghana, Sudan and Togo, but is from Cameroon we take this dish, where it is popular as a street food and can be served with a variety of accompaniments, including spicy sauces.

In this recipe we are serving the Suya with another West African favourite, Jelouf Rice.

## What you need

### For the beef

1 kg beef steak, 12 pieces
150 g peanuts, finely crushed
1 tbs ground cinnamon
1 tbs garlic powder
1 tbs ground ginger
1 tbs cayenne pepper
1 tbs ground smoked paprika
1 tbs chilli powder
2 tsp onion salt
vegetable oil, for drizzling

## What to do

Cut the steak into long strips, approximately 2 cm wide. In a shallow dish, mix together the peanuts, cinnamon, garlic, ginger, cayenne, paprika, chilli and onion salt. Combine well.
Roll the strips of steak in the mixture, covering well. Press the mixture well into the meat. Leave to marinate for 1-2 hours in the fridge.
Soak bamboo skewers in water for 20 minutes. Thread the meat onto the skewers in a spiral. Drizzle with oil and grill on a medium heat to taste.

## What you need

### For the rice

300 g long-grain rice
2 carrots, sliced
10 green beans, sliced
1 large onion, sliced
3 tbs each, chopped leek, parsley and celery
1 small chilli, finely chopped (optional)
4 tomatoes, sliced
1 tsp salt
1 stock cube (beef or vegetable)
50 ml groundnut oil

# 10 - Suya and Jelouf Rice - Cameroon

**What to do**

Boil the unwashed rice for 25 minutes, then drain and wash in cold water.

Put the oil into a large pan then add the rice and all the remaining ingredients. Mix well. Add 300 ml of water. Cover the pan and bring to the boil. Simmer on a low heat for 25 minutes. Check to see if the water has been absorbed and the rice is cooked.

Allow to stand for 10 minutes with the lid on. Gently stir the rice to mix well before serving with the Suya.

# 11 - Banana and Date Mix - Burundi

Burundi, in Central Africa has been in existence for some 500 years. The Tutsi ruled the country for over 200 years until the early 20$^{th}$ century, when the country was occupied by both Germany and Belgium. In the middle part of the 20$^{th}$ century, differences between the Tutsi and the Hutu boiled over into a civil war.

Around 80% of the land in Burundi is given over to agriculture. Tea, coffee, corn, manioc (cassava) and beans. Burundi cuisine is very typical of African culinary culture; beans being a staple food. Meat production is secondary, and although sheep and goat do feature in some recipes, the majority centre around fruit and vegetables and pulses.

A further influence on Burundi cuisine is the poor economic situation in the country, the food is usually homemade and homemade vessels are used for drinking, storing and carrying food and water.

Occasionally a recipe comes to light that is so simple, yet so tasty that you wonder where it has been all your life. This offering from Burundi is one such recipe.

## What you need

110 g butter
85 g sugar
2 eggs
135 g flour
1 pinch salt
2 tsp baking powder
4 bananas, sliced
125 g dates, chopped
10 g butter, melted
1 tsp cinnamon powder
2 tbs sugar

## What to do

Preheat the oven to 180°C.

Cream together the butter and sugar. Add the eggs, flour, salt and baking powder. Mix well. Transfer half the mixture to a baking dish and mould into place.

Place the bananas and dates on the mixture then cover with the remaining mixture. This is quite difficult as the dough is sticky and will refuse to come off the spoon or your fingers. Bake for 30 minutes, or until the top turns a golden brown.

While it is cooking, mix together the cinnamon and the 2 tbs of sugar.

When cooked, remove from the oven and brush with melted butter. Sprinkle with the sugar and cinnamon mixture.

Serve warm.

## Cook's tip:

If you have a member of the family who is allergic to, or doesn't like, bananas, these can be substituted with apple, which is as equally delicious.

# 12 - Kuku Wa Kupaka - Kenya

In 1496, the Portuguese arrived on the coast of Kenya, and introduced new foods from Brazil such as maize, bananas, pineapple, chillies, peppers, sweet potato and cassava. They also brought oranges, lemons, and limes from China and India.

Raising cattle has a long history in Kenya, and by the 1600s, groups like the Maasai and Turkana ate beef exclusively.

Other Europeans countries brought white potatoes, cucumbers, and tomatoes. The British brought with them many Indian labourers which in turn led to the introduction of curries, chapattis and chutneys to the cuisine and these became a traditional Sunday lunch for many Kenyan families.

The society is multiracial, comprising mainly of native ethnic groups, the majority of the rest being a mixture of Asians, Arabs and Europeans. As would be expected, this mix of races and nationalities has influenced the cuisine.

Most dishes are filling and inexpensive to make, using staple foods consisting mainly of corn, potatoes, and beans.

This particular dish is from the Kenyan coastal regions.

## What you need

8-10 chicken breasts/thighs
large piece fresh ginger, peeled and finely chopped
5 cloves of garlic, finely chopped
1 tsp fresh rosemary
3 green chillies, finely chopped
juice of one lime
3 tbs vegetable oil
1 onion, finely chopped
2 fresh tomatoes, sliced
1 tsp tomato purée
1 tsp turmeric
1 tsp cumin seeds
500 ml coconut cream
salt and freshly ground pepper to taste
fresh coriander, chopped (optional)

## What to do

Marinate the chicken in the ginger, garlic, rosemary, chillies, lime juice, salt and 1 tsp vegetable oil. Cover and refrigerate for 12 hours.

Remove the chicken after marinating. Set aside the remaining marinade for use later.

Grill the chicken or bake in the oven for 30 minutes. The chicken should be just cooked.

Heat the remaining vegetable oil in a large pan. Sauté the onions until lightly browned. Add the sliced tomatoes then simmer on a medium heat for 2-3 minutes. Stir in tomato purée and cook for a further minute. Add the turmeric and cumin seeds, stir and mix thoroughly for 5 minutes. Add the coconut milk and the remaining marinade set aside from the chicken.

Lower the heat and stir the sauce for about 5 minutes until thick.

Season to taste. Add the grilled chicken to the pan, cover and simmer for 30 minutes until the chicken is tender.

Alternatively, place the chicken in an ovenproof serving dish, pour the sauce over the chicken and cook at 180°C for 30 minutes. Check frequently while cooking.

Garnish with fresh chopped coriander (optional). Serve with rice.

## 12 - Kuku Wa Kupaka - Kenya

# 13 - Bolo Polana - Mozambique

Much African cooking has been influenced by colonisation and trading. This is particularly so in Mozambique which has been influenced by Arab, Persian, and later Portuguese, slave and precious metal traders, not to mention the Indian spice traders. Of these, the Portuguese have had by far the biggest influence on the region, settling there from the late 15$^{th}$ century.

Without these influences, this recipe would be missing the two main ingredients, potatoes and cashews, both of which were at one time only found in South America. They were almost certainly introduced to Mozambique by the Portuguese.

These days, Bolo Polana is considered to be a traditional Mozambican dessert and the named comes from the Polana district of the Mozambican capital, Maputo. The combination of cashews and potatoes produces a rich cake with a nutty flavour.

## What you need

500 g potatoes, peeled
500 g raw, unsalted cashew nuts
2 tbs flour
400 g sugar
220 g butter
peel from 2 lemons, grated
9 egg yolks
4 egg whites, beaten

## What to do

Bring the potatoes to a boil in a saucepan, then simmer for 20 minutes until soft.
While the potatoes are cooking either bake the cashews for 15 minutes at 170°C until slightly browned or toast them in a dry frying pan. Process the cashews in a food processor until they form a smooth paste then set aside in a bowl.
Once the potatoes are cooked, mash them well so they are creamy, then combine with the nuts. Add the flour, sugar, butter and lemon peel to a food processor and blend until light and creamy. Add to the potato and nut mixture. To this mixture add the egg yolks one by one, mixing constantly. Add egg whites to the mixture and combine well.
Pour the mixture into a greased cake tin and bake at 180°C for 30-45 minutes until the top is golden brown and the centre of the cake is cooked.
Allow to cool for 10 minutes before removing from the cake tin.
Serve when cool.

## Cook's tip:

To test if a cake is cooked in the middle, insert a meat skewer into the centre of the cake. If any mixture is clinging to the skewer when you withdraw it, the cake needs more time in the oven.

# 13 - Bolo Polana - Mozambique

# 14 - Curried Gazelle - Zambia

The Zambian diet centres predominantly around cereals, particularly maize (sweetcorn) which is ground to produce nshima, a stiff porridge. This can be eaten as a thin porridge for breakfast and made thicker for lunch and dinner, sometimes dipped in a relish of meat, vegetables or fish. Other local dishes include ifisashi, which is made from green vegetables in a peanut sauce, and samp, made from crushed maize and beans. Livestock production is low, so meat is not a regular feature in Zambian cuisine, but wildlife abounds and occasionally appears on the table.

## What you need

1 kg gazelle rump steaks (or venison rump) cut into bite size cubes **(see Cook's tip)**
1 tbs vegetable oil
2 onions, chopped
3 garlic cloves, chopped
2 large chillies, finely chopped (I used one Habanero which was quite hot enough)
2 plantains, peeled and sliced (banana can be used)
1 tbs tomato paste
1 tbs raisins
2 tsp curry powder
1 tsp ground cumin
1 tsp ground cardamom
½ tsp ground turmeric
½ tsp paprika
300 ml coconut milk

## What to do

In a large saucepan, lightly fry the onion in the oil for 3 minutes. Add the garlic and fry for 1 more minute before adding the chillies. Cook for a further 3 minutes then add the meat and brown on all sides.
Once browned add the tomato paste, raisins, curry powder and spices. Stir and cook for a minute then add the coconut milk and bring to a boil. Reduce to a simmer and add the sliced plantains. Cover and simmer gently for a further 30 minutes (check occasionally to ensure the mixture is not too dry. Add a little water if you need to).
Serve immediately on a bed of rice.

## Cook's tip:

The chances of obtaining gazelle meat outside Africa are slim, even venison can be hard to come by in certain areas. Some versions of this dish suggest substituting beef, lamb or goat. Venison is a very lean meat so to replicate this recipe as closely as possible using local ingredients, and if venison isn't available, then you should choose a very lean cut of beef. In this case, South African Topside was used. Both goat and lamb are quite fatty, and while either can be used to make an excellent curry, I would not choose to use them in this recipe.

## 14 - Curried Gazelle - Zambia

# 15 - Ginger and Quince Stew - Namibia

Like many African countries, Namibia has a mixed past and was colonised by Germany in the latter part of the 19th century. German rule ended in 1915 after South Africa defeated the German military forces. In 1920, the League of Nations mandated the country to the United Kingdom, under administration by South Africa and it gained its independence in 1990.

It would be easy to imagine Namibia to be a poor country, but this is not the case. Namibia has gem, diamond and uranium deposits, as well as number of other minerals such as tungsten, gold, copper and zinc, to name a few. Yet it is one of the least densely populated countries in the world; over 20% of the country is desert. Despite this, agriculture is strong.

Much of the population relies on subsistence farming, although there are some 4,000 commercial livestock producing farms. Crop growing is restricted to approximately 2% of the land as the rainfall in much of the country is too low for commercial crop growing. Goat farming takes place mainly in the arid south of the country. The Boer goat is indigenous to Africa, with both South African and Namibian breeders contributing to making it one of the best breeds of goat in the world.

## What you need

1.5 kg Boerbok neck and/or shoulder cut into pieces (good quality goat is fine)
2 tsp ground nutmeg
½ tsp ground cloves
salt and freshly ground black pepper
2 tbs oil
2 large onions, chopped
6 cloves garlic, peeled and crushed
1 piece (5 cm) root ginger, sliced
1.5 kg quinces, peeled, sliced and covered with lemon water **(see Cook's tip)**
1 tsp ground turmeric
1 tsp ground ginger
1 tsp ground pimento
1 piece cinnamon

## What to do

Mix the nutmeg, cloves, salt and pepper with the meat. Heat a little oil in a heavy-bottomed saucepan and brown a few pieces of meat at a time.

Cook the onions, garlic and root ginger in the same saucepan in which the meat was browned and fry until tender. Put half of the meat back into the saucepan combining well with the onion mixture. Drain the quinces and flavour with the turmeric, ginger and pimento. Place half of the quinces, together with the cinnamon stick, onto the meat in the saucepan. Cover with the remaining meat, topping off with the rest of the quinces. Add a little water, bring to the boil then reduce the heat and simmer for 2 hours. Check frequently, adding more liquid if necessary.

## Cook's tip:

If you are unable to obtain quinces, then you can substitute with Bartlett pears or a firm apple such as Granny Smith or Golden Delicious.

## 15 - Ginger and Quince Stew - Namibia

# 16 - Bobotie - South Africa

When it comes to the number one melting pot of cultures, South Africa must be one of the top candidates for the prize.

South Africa was colonised by the Dutch in the mid 17th century, followed by the Germans, French, Italians and British, all of whom had presence in the country. Then there are the people the colonists brought in, such as the Cape Malays. Further influences can be found from neighbouring countries, such as Mozambique, which itself was heavily influenced by the Portuguese.

Then of course, there are the indigenous people of Africa, all of whom brought their own ingredients and brand of cooking to the region.

Now stir this all together, along with the inevitable spices brought from the Far East, and we come up with a recipe such as this.

The origins of this dish can probably be traced back even earlier than the mid 17th century, possibly as far back as the days of the Roman Empire, but the dish as presented here is definitely a product of Africa, not Rome, and is virtually the national dish of South Africa.

## What you need

2 slices white bread
2 onions, chopped
25 g butter
2 garlic cloves, crushed
1 kg lean minced beef
2 tbs madras curry paste
1 tsp dried mixed herbs
3 cloves
5 allspice berries
2 tbs mango chutney
3 tbs sultanas
1 tsp salt
6 bay leaves
ground pepper
300 ml full-cream milk
2 large eggs

## What to do

Heat the oven to 180°C.
Soak the bread in cold water.
In a large frying pan, fry the onions in the butter for 10 minutes until soft and starting to colour. Add the garlic and minced beef and stir well. Break up the mince and cook until browned. Add the curry paste, herbs, spices, chutney, sultanas, salt and 2 of the bay leaves, with plenty of freshly ground black pepper. Mix well, then cover and simmer for 10 minutes.
Squeeze the excess water from the bread, then beat it into the meat mixture until well blended. Place in a deep ovenproof dish. Press the mixture down well and ensure the top is smooth.
Beat the eggs with the milk and add seasoning. Pour over the meat. Top with the remaining bay leaves and bake for 35-40 minutes until the topping has set and is starting to turn golden.
Serve with crusty bread or rice.

## Cook's tip:

This dish is suitable to be made a day ahead and chilled. Ensure it is reheated thoroughly before serving.

# 16 - Bobotie - South Africa

# 17 - Veal Chops in Green Peppercorn Sauce - Madagascar

Ranked as the fourth largest island in the world (Australia is excluded as it is considered to be a continent), Madagascar saw its first settlers some 2,000 years ago. This makes it a relative latecomer in the world of human habitation. The early settlers were thought to be from Borneo, followed later by people from Africa. Madagascar came under French colonisation in the late 19$^{th}$ century, and more recently there have been settlers from China and India.

The staple food of the Malagasy (natives of Madagascar) is rice, and this forms the basis for most dishes. Often in rural areas of the arid south and west, the rice will be substituted with maize, cassava or curds made from the milk of the zebu, a breed of cattle originating in South Asia. An accompaniment of vegetables or meat is used with the rice, and they typically feature a sauce which can be flavoured with ginger, garlic, onion, tomato, curry powder, or other spices or herbs. Malagasy cuisine can be traditional, as would have been prepared by the early settlers or the more contemporary cuisine which reflects the variety of settlers in this land.

## What you need

4 veal chops (steaks can be used)
salt and black pepper
2 tbs butter
1 tbs olive oil
2 tbs green peppercorns in brine, drained
2 tbs apple juice
50 ml chicken stock (make up 500 ml from a stockpot and freeze the rest)
120 ml double cream

## What to do

Preheat the oven to 200°C.
Season the veal chops with salt.
Heat the butter and the olive oil in a large frying pan until very hot then add the veal chops. Brown on both sides. When browned, transfer to a shallow ovenproof dish using a pair of tongs or a slotted spoon, and roast in the oven for 10 minutes.
Meanwhile add the green peppercorns to the remaining juices in the frying pan, stirring over a low heat. Add the apple juice and stock, then bring to the boil, stirring for 1 minute.
Add the cream, mix well then continue to cook for 3-4 minutes until the sauce thickens.
Season the sauce to taste, then pour over the cooked veal chops. Serve immediately with steamed rice.

## 17 - Veal Chops in Green Peppercorn Sauce - Madagascar

# 18 - Laghman - Kyrgyzstan

Traditionally the Kyrgyz people were nomadic and so the preparation and ingredients involved Kyrgyz cuisine are centred around the long-term preservation of the food. As would be expected from a nomadic lifestyle, meat features strongly in the recipes, although vegetables are surprisingly common in Kyrgyz dishes.

As with much of Central Asia, other common ingredients are dumplings and noodles. Making a simple dough for noodles would be an easy task for the nomadic people and form a filling addition to any meal.

Laghman is a very popular dish in Kyrgyzstan, although strictly speaking it comes from the Dungan or Uyghur ethnic groups within the Kyrgyz peoples.

## What you need

### For the noodles

500 g flour
1 egg
1 tsp salt
60 ml water

### For the broth

300 g fat, cubed **(see Cook's tip)**
3 onions, cut into rings
500 g lamb, cubed
3 potatoes, cubed
1 carrot, sliced
3 tomatoes, cut into wedges
6 cloves garlic, finely chopped
1 red chilli, finely chopped
2 peppers, thinly sliced
300 g cabbage, thinly sliced
salt and pepper to taste

## What to do

Melt the fat in a large saucepan and sauté the onion. Add the meat and brown well. Add the potatoes, carrot, tomatoes, garlic, chilli and peppers. Stir well and cook until about half-done (4-5 minutes). Add enough water to cover the meat and vegetables and add the salt, pepper, and cabbage. Cook over a low heat until thoroughly cooked (about an hour).

Meanwhile, mix together the flour, egg, salt and water as necessary. Ensure the dough is stiff, not too wet and not too dry. Roll out until it forms a thin sheet. Roll the dough as if rolling up a sheet of paper, then slice across to make narrow noodles about 4-5 mm thick. Drop into boiling salted water and cook until done, 3-4 minutes. Drain well.

If this is done towards the end of the cooking time for the broth it won't be necessary to reheat the noodles, but if they get too cold, reheat by dropping briefly into boiling water.

To serve, spoon the mixture over the noodles, allowing the liquid to soak through.

## Cook's tip:

Traditionally the fat comes from the tail, but any fat is acceptable.

## 18 - Laghman - Kyrgyzstan

# 19 - Khuushuur - Mongolia

In common with the Kyrgyz, the Mongols are traditionally a nomadic people, living by raising animals and moving from place to place wherever the conditions are best for the livestock. Vegetarians will struggle here as vegetables do not feature widely in Mongolian cooking. A high fat content in the food allows the Mongols to live in the harsh conditions that are often a feature of their nomadic lifestyle.

As mentioned elsewhere in this book, people often don't recognise the borders determined by politics. Similar dishes are often seen in adjacent countries and so there are similarities between the dishes of Mongolia, the adjacent regions of Russia and China and indeed many of the countries of this part of Asia.

Buuz and Banshur, both of which are steamed dumplings, and Khuushuur, which is fried, are considered to be a form of fast food in Mongolia and can often be found served together in the restaurants of Ulaanbaatar, the capital of Mongolia.

## What you need

### For the dough

250 g flour
150 ml water

### For the filling

300 g minced mutton or lamb
1 onion, finely chopped
2 garlic cloves, finely chopped
1 tsp caraway seeds
3-5 tbs water
salt and pepper to taste

## What to do

Mix the flour and water to form a dough. Only add enough water to make the dough smooth. If it is too wet add some more flour.
Let the dough rest for 15 minutes.
Mix together the minced lamb, onion, garlic, caraway seeds and enough water to form a smooth mixture.
Roll the dough to form one long sausage 3 cm thick. Cut into 4 cm lengths, then flatten each piece with your fingers. Roll each piece into a 10 cm circle, slightly thicker in the middle than the edges. Only roll as many as you can deal with in a few minutes.
Take a disc in the palm of one hand and place about 1½ tsp of the filling on one half, then fold the other half over using the fingers and your palm to form a half moon. Press the two edges together to seal the pocket.
In Mongolia, the cooks take great pride in decorating the edge into fancy patterns, but it will be sufficient to scallop the edges for your first few attempts. From the photographs, you can clearly see I am not a Mongolian cook!
Deep fry in hot oil until golden. Take care when cooking as some of the liquid from the filling can escape and cause the oil to splash.
Serve with ketchup or chilli sauce for a complete meal.

## 19 - Khuushuur - Mongolia

# 20 - Black Bread - Russia

Black bread has a strong association with the Russian peasantry and historically has been more prevalent than white bread. The colder temperatures of Russia are more suited to growing rye than wheat and so rye flour was easier and cheaper to obtain. Even so, Kings and Generals, who could afford the more expensive and harder to obtain white bread, often ate black bread because of its association with the values of the Russian peasantry.

## What you need

400 g rye flour
375 g white flour
1 tsp sugar
2 tsp salt
100 g whole bran cereal
2 tsp instant coffee
2 tsp onion powder
2 tbs caraway seed, crushed
½ tsp fennel seed, crushed
2 packets active dry yeast
600 ml water
60 ml vinegar (or 30 ml balsamic vinegar)
60 ml dark molasses
1 square unsweetened chocolate or 1 tsp cocoa
55 g butter

## What to do

Mix together the rye and white flour. Add the sugar, salt, cereal, coffee, onion powder, caraway seed, fennel seed and dry yeast.
In a saucepan, combine the water, vinegar, molasses, chocolate and butter.
Using a low heat, heat until the liquids are warm (don't worry about the butter and chocolate melting, it isn't necessary).
Gradually add the liquid to the dry ingredients until a soft dough is formed (you may not have to use all the liquid). Work the dough to ensure all the ingredients are combined well.
Turn the dough out onto a lightly floured board. Cover and let it rest for about 15 minutes, then knead until smooth and elastic (this is a good workout for the arm muscles). Well-kneaded dough has a sheen to it as the gluten is formed and will take about 10-15 minutes. The dough may still be a little sticky at this stage.
Place the dough in a greased bowl, turning to grease the top of the dough as well as the bottom. Cover and let it rise in a warm place, free from any draught.
The oven is a suitable place, but if you are using an electric oven ensure the fan is turned off. Set the temperature to the lowest setting and keep the door closed.
When the dough has doubled in bulk (about an hour), punch it down and turn out onto a lightly floured board. Divide in half.
Shape each half into a ball about 12 cm across. Place each ball into the centre of a greased 20 cm round cake tin or use a 900 g loaf tin.
Cover, and let it rise in the same warm place until they're both doubled in bulk again.
Bake at 180°C for 45-50 minutes or until done.
Remove from the tins and cool on wire racks.

# 20 - Black Bread - Russia

# 21 - Shandong Chicken - China

The Shandong province has played a major role in both the history and cuisine of China. It is situated in the eastern part of the country (the name translates as 'east of the mountains') and on the intersection of both ancient and modern, north-south and east-west trade routes. As we have already seen in both Middle-Eastern and African cuisine, these trades routes were the means by which new ingredients and cooking methods were spread, so it is not surprising the Shandong province is considered to be one of the most influential in Chinese cooking.

Outside China, we tend to see food from the southern provinces, so you won't often see Shandong dishes on the menu in a Chinese restaurant. However, many of the dishes you do see will have been influenced by the Shandong style.

A wide variety of ingredients and cooking methods are used, and with a 3,000 km coastline it is not surprising one of the major ingredients is seafood, but it is from the land we will take our ingredients for this easy to make chicken dish.

## What you need

2 tbs melted butter
120 ml mayonnaise
2 tbs prepared horseradish
1 tbs white sugar
¾ tsp ground black pepper
1 pinch salt
120 ml white vinegar
60 ml cup water
4 chicken leg quarters

## How to make

Preheat the oven to 175°C.
Line a baking sheet or tin with foil, and brush with the melted butter.
Mix together the horseradish, mayonnaise, sugar, salt and pepper in a bowl, then slowly add the vinegar and water. Mix until well blended.
Coat each piece of chicken heavily with the sauce, and place onto the prepared baking sheet.
Bake, uncovered, for about 45 minutes, basting occasionally with remaining sauce.
The chicken is done when the juices run clear, and the meat is no longer pink.
Serve with steamed rice or noodles.

## Cook's tip:

Prepare the day before and allow the chicken to marinate in the sauce overnight before cooking for a stronger taste.
When marinating slice diagonally into the skin and flesh of the meat to allow better penetration of the marinade.

## 21 - Shandong Chicken - China

# 22 - Tempura - Japan

When we think of Japanese food, we tend to think of sushi and noodles, but Japanese cuisine is far more than that. In Japan, preparation is an art form, and the food tends to be exquisitely prepared and presented, with chefs honing their preparation skills over many years.

As would be expected from an island nation, fish features heavily in the recipes of Japan, and it is from the sea we have taken the main ingredient for this dish.

## What you need

### For the assorted Tempura

8 raw tiger prawns, cleaned and shelled but with tail intact
flour, for coating
½ squid body cut into 3 cm strips or 20 squid rings
115 g sweet potato
75 g carrot, cut into matchsticks
4 shiitake mushrooms, stems removed
50 French beans, trimmed
1 red pepper, seeded and sliced into 2 cm strips
1 small aubergine, sliced into 5 mm discs
2 packets Tempura batter mix **(see Cook's tip)**

### For the dip (mix all ingredients together)

200 ml water
3 tbs soy sauce
3 tbs rice wine vinegar
*1 shiitake mushroom thinly sliced
*1 small sheet kombu seaweed (sliced)
(* These items can be replaced by 6 g bonito flakes if available)

### For the rice

6 dried shiitake mushrooms
800 ml water
2 sheets fried tofu 13x6 cm or fresh firm tofu for frying
6 mangetout
1 carrot, cut into matchsticks
115 g chicken breast, diced
2 tbs sugar
7 tsp soy sauce
450 g Japonica rice
salt to taste

## What to do

### For the Tempura

Soak the sweet potato, sliced but unpeeled, for 5 minutes in cold water.
Put the ingredients for the dip into a saucepan and bring to the boil. Remove from the heat, allow to cool then strain. Divide between bowls for the number of diners.
Make diagonal slits in the prawn tails, cutting into about ⅔ of the way.
Make the batter according to the instructions on the packet.
Heat oil in a pan or deep fat fryer to 185°C.
Dust the prawns lightly with the flour then dip into the batter mix. Lower gently into the oil and cook until crisp but not quite golden.
Repeat for the squid.
Dip the vegetables directly into the batter and cook in the same way. The beans and carrot strips can be placed in small bunches to dip.
Dip only the undersides of the mushrooms.
Drain well.
The tempura mix can be kept warm in an oven preheated to 100°C but it is better to serve as soon as possible.

# 22 - Tempura - Japan

**For the rice**

Soak the mushrooms in the water for 30 minutes.

Meanwhile cook the rice and keep warm.

If using fried tofu sheets, put into a strainer and put hot water over them. Squeeze, then cut the sheets in half then into 5 mm strips. If using fresh tofu, shave slices of tofu from the block, then deep fry until crisp. Prepare as for ready fried sheets.

Boil the mangetout until just tender, drain and refresh in cold water. Shred finely.

Drain the mushrooms reserving the liquid. Remove and discard the stems then finely slice the mushrooms.

Put the reserved liquid into a pan with the carrot, chicken, mushroom and tofu. Bring to the boil, then skim the broth. Simmer for 2-3 minutes then add the sugar and cook for a further minute. Add the soy and salt.

Simmer until almost all the water has evaporated, leaving a concentrated broth. Add the hot boiled rice, mix thoroughly. Sprinkle the mangetout over the rice and serve.

**Cook's tip:**

Whilst it is easy to make your own tempura batter, it is more convenient to buy a ready-made mix. If you seek true authenticity, then there are numerous recipes online to make your own.

# 23 - Spinach Soup, Fried Fish, Rice with Mushrooms - Korea

Korean cuisine is largely based on rice, meat and vegetables. From what was essentially both a nomadic and agricultural society, the food has undergone many changes over the centuries. What were originally regional dishes, became adopted nationally as the nomadic people moved through the country. The spread of these regional dishes was aided by the Royal Court of the Joseon Dynasty, which ruled Korea from 1392 until 1910. The Royal Court took dishes from all the regions and showcased them in a style of cooking named after the Royal Court, in which the tradition is to serve 12 dishes along with rice and soup.

We are not going to cook 12 dishes in this recipe, but we are going to make a starter, a main course and a rice dish.

## What you need

### For the soup

125 g steak
2 spring onions, chopped
1 garlic clove, finely chopped
1 tbs sesame seeds
750 ml water
225 g spinach
1 tbs dark soy sauce
salt to taste

### For the fish

675 g white fish fillets
2 tbs light soy sauce
salt
pepper, freshly ground
2 spring onions, chopped
groundnut oil
2 large tomatoes, skinned
12 lettuce leaves
1 onion, cut into rings

### For the rice

225 g mushrooms
225 g lean beef
2 tbs groundnut oil
2 chopped onions
225 g long-grain rice
500 ml boiling water
salt to taste
pepper, freshly ground
2 tbs light soy sauce
2 tbs lightly roasted sesame seeds

## What to do

### For the soup

Dry the meat on kitchen paper and cut into thin slices, then into strips and finally into pieces.

# 23 - Spinach Soup, Fried Fish, Rice with Mushrooms - Korea

Dry fry the meat, spring onions, garlic and sesame seeds in a hot wok for 1 minute, stirring constantly.
Add the water, stir well, bring to the boil then simmer on a reduced heat for 10 minutes.
Wash the spinach and cut into narrow strips.
Add the spinach and salt to taste. Stir in the soy sauce and remove from the heat.
Serve in warmed bowls.

### For the fish

Rinse the fish, then dry and cut into 12 equal pieces.
Mix the soy sauce, spring onions, salt and pepper in a bowl. Add the fish and ensure well coated with the marinade. Leave to marinate for at least 15 minutes.
Cut each tomato into 6 slices. Place the lettuce leaves on a cold plate and put some onion rings and a slice of tomato on each.
Remove the fish and dry with kitchen roll.
Heat the oil in a wok and fry the pieces until golden then place on the lettuce leaves.
Serve immediately.

### For the rice

Slice the mushrooms and cut into thin strips.
Dry the meat then cut into 5 mm slices, then into strips.
Heat the oil in a wok and stir-fry the meat, mushrooms and onions for 3 minutes.
Add the rice and stir continuously for 2 minutes. Add the boiling water, salt to taste, a little pepper and the soy sauce. Stir several times and bring to the boil. Reduce the heat, cover and simmer for 20 minutes. Keep the lid on the wok until just before serving. Stir with a fork and transfer to a warmed dish. Sprinkle with the sesame seeds.

# 24 - Sichuan Chicken Stir-Fry - China

For those who have had any contact with Chinese cooking, any reference to Sichuan cuisine is likely to bring thoughts of fiery, spicy dishes. But, there should be much more to any spicy cooking than pure heat. The aim is to create a balance of ingredients and spices.

The Sichuan district of China was already blessed with the Sichuan peppercorn, which is actually the berry of the prickly ash tree and has a touch of lemon in the flavour. Then, in the 16th century, chillies arrived from South America, courtesy of the Portuguese, and these were soon incorporated into Sichuan cuisine.

When used correctly, the Sichuan peppercorn will produce a tingling sensation to the palate but overdo it and you will end up with a numb tongue and lips.

The fieriness of the chilli and the heat from the peppercorn sit well with ginger and garlic which are used extensively. In this dish we add onions, peppers, fresh green broccoli and salty soy sauce into the mix.

Think of carnivals and fiestas, and your thoughts will turn to bright colours and lively music. Sichuan cuisine is a carnival for the taste buds, bringing a riot of flavours that should tease and surprise with every mouthful.

**Cook's tip:**

Stir fry dishes are cooked in a relatively short time; most of the time spent in the kitchen is on preparation. Make sure all your ingredients are ready before you start cooking; you won't have time to slice peppers or peel onions once things are underway.

**What you need**

1 tbs Sichuan peppercorns
salt to taste
450 g boneless, skinless chicken, pounded thin and cut into 2.5 cm thick strips
2 tbs groundnut oil
5 cm piece ginger, minced
3 garlic cloves, minced
1 large onion, julienned
350 g broccoli florets
1 green pepper, julienned
1 red pepper, julienned
1 yellow pepper, julienned
4 shiitake mushrooms, sliced thinly
2 tbs light soy sauce
25 ml apple cider vinegar
25 ml water
3 red chillies, minced
3 spring onions, thinly cut, diagonally

**What to do**

If using dried shiitake mushrooms, place them in a bowl of water for 15 minutes before slicing.
Toast the Sichuan peppercorns in a small, dry saucepan, until fragrant. Remove from the heat and grind the peppercorns in a spice grinder. Season the chicken pieces with the peppercorns and salt and set aside for 15 minutes.
Heat a large wok over high heat. Add 1 tbs of oil and stir-fry the chicken until almost cooked. Remove and set aside.
Add the remaining oil to the wok then add the ginger, garlic and onions. Stir fry for 1 minute. Add the broccoli, peppers, shiitake mushrooms, soy sauce, vinegar, water and chillies. Stir-fry for

# 24 - Sichuan Chicken Stir-Fry - China

2 minutes. Add the chicken and stir-fry for 1 minute. Add the spring onions and stir-fry for a further minute. Ensure the chicken is cooked through, then serve with rice or noodles.

# 25 - Aaloo Dam - Nepal

Many times, in this book, we see how the cuisine of a country is a melting pot of influences, both regional and international. These influences come about as people from other countries and continents bring a variety of ingredients and cooking methods with them, and to a degree it is the same with Nepal. This mountainous country differs from some of the others we see in this book, because Nepal only opened its borders to outsiders during the 1950s and the greatest influences are from its closest geographical neighbours such as China, India and Tibet. Combine this with the transport and trade difficulties caused by Nepal's geographical setting, Nepalese cuisine maintains a focus on using locally grown produce.

Relying less on using fats and more on chunky vegetables, lean meats, pickles and salads, Nepalese cooking is generally considered to be healthier than most other South-Asian cuisine.

Common ingredients include; chillies, coriander, cumin, garlic, lentils, mustard oil, peppers, potatoes, and tomatoes.

**What you need**

1 kg small potatoes
¼ tsp fenugreek seed
1 large onion, chopped
125 g/120 ml plain yoghurt
1 tbs cashew nut pieces or paste (optional)
1 tsp ginger paste
1 tsp garlic paste
1 tsp red chilli powder
1 tsp ground coriander
1 tsp ground turmeric
1 tsp garam masala
2 large tomatoes, chopped
230 ml water
oil for deep frying
salt to taste

**What to do**

Par-boil the unpeeled potatoes for 5-10 minutes until half cooked. Allow to cool.
Peel, then prick the potatoes with a fork. Deep fry until golden brown.
Heat 2 tsp of oil in another pan. Add the fenugreek seed and fry until they start to turn dark. Add the onion and cook until light brown.
Stir in the yoghurt, cashew nuts, ginger paste, garlic paste, red chilli powder, ground coriander, ground turmeric and garam masala.
Stir in the tomato and cook on a medium heat for few minutes.
Add the water and salt to taste. Bring to the boil. Add the fried potatoes and cook for 8-10 minutes on low heat.

For a traditional dish serve with Nepal Pulao rice and/or Roti or serve with the rice and naan of your choice.

# 26 - Ema Datshi - Bhutan

Bhutan is a Kingdom in the Himalayas, bordered by China to the North and India to the south, east and west. It is not so surprising to discover the country's cuisine is influenced by Indian, Chinese and Tibetan culture. Unlike Nepal, which until recently remained relatively isolated, Bhutan had regular contact with other cultures via the Silk Road, the ancient trade route linking Asia with the West.

The main dish of a meal, generally includes white or red rice, seasonal vegetables, and meat and is often cooked with chilli or cheese.

Ema Datshi is the National Dish of Bhutan. A spicy mix of chillies (ema), and the local cheese known as Datshi. This dish is a staple of nearly every meal in Bhutan and can be found throughout the country. Variations on Ema Datshi include adding vegetables such as green beans, potatoes or mushrooms, or swapping the regular cheese for yak cheese.

As would be expected from a dish whose main ingredient is chilli, it is quite hot. If you wish for a slightly milder version, remove the seeds and membranes from the chillies before adding to the pan.

## What you need

250 g chillies, Jalapeño or similar
1 onion, thinly sliced
2 tsp vegetable oil
400 ml water
2 medium or 1 large tomato, diced
5 garlic cloves, finely crushed
250 g Feta cheese
3 coriander leaves

## What to do

Slice each chilli lengthways into 4 pieces. Add the vegetable oil to the water in a pan, along with the chillies and onions. Bring to the boil and simmer over a medium heat for 10 minutes.

Add the tomato and garlic and simmer for another 2 minutes.

Add the cheese and simmer for a further 2-3 minutes. Finally add the coriander and turn off the heat. Stir.

Keep the pan covered and let stand for 2 minutes.

Serve with a generous portion of red rice or polished white rice, along with side dishes.

## Cook's tip:

The cheese that is normally used to create this dish cannot be found outside Bhutan. Usually made by local farmers, Datshi cheese has a unique texture and doesn't dissolve in boiling water.

## 26 - Ema Datshi - Bhutan

# 27 - Split Pea Fritters (Beya Kya) - Myanmar

Rice cultivation has been practised for centuries in Myanmar (formerly Burma) owing to the presence of three major rivers, the Irrawaddy, the Chindwin and the Salween, which have been an important source of irrigation throughout the central region and was a staple for early settlers. These rivers and the coastal areas also provided fish and shellfish as important protein in the early diets. In the forested highlands where the climate is dry and little arable land available, the people traditionally relied on a mixture of hunting, gathering, and dry-rice farming and practiced "slash-and-burn" cultivation. With the colonisation by the British in the mid 19$^{th}$ century, and the incorporation of the country into British India, Indians arrived and established firm culinary traditions in the area. At the same time, Chinese settlers came, bringing their own influences on the cuisine. These are still evident today in the use of noodles and soy sauce and the making of curries, albeit less spicy than the Indian varieties. Thai influences can also be seen in the use of lemongrass, fish sauce and coconut.

A cross between Chinese and Thai food with some Indian influence is probably the best way to describe the cuisine of this land; richer than Chinese but not as spicy as Thai or Indian. The country's major agricultural staple remains rice, which is served at every meal, usually boiled. Beans, pulses and noodles are also frequent visitors to the table. Common ingredients are garlic, ginger, turmeric, chillies, onions and shrimp paste.

This recipe is a snack which is easy to make and can be altered to suit your taste. It could be used as part of a main course and although not strictly Burmese, it is delicious with a sweet chilli garlic dip.

## What you need

225 g split peas (I used chickpeas, but other types could be used)
1 large onion, finely chopped
2 fresh red chillies, finely chopped, or ¼ tsp chilli powder (more if you like it spicy)
½ tsp ground turmeric
½ tsp salt
oil for deep frying
sliced onion and lemon wedges to garnish

## What to do

Soak split peas in water overnight, or for at least 6 hours.
Drain, grind to a paste in blender or put twice through fine screen of mincer.
Mix remaining ingredients except the oil.
In your hands make small balls of mixture then flatten to about 10 mm thickness.
Heat oil in deep frying pan or wok and fry the fritters one at a time until golden brown.
Drain on absorbent paper.
Serve garnished with sliced raw onion and lemon wedges.

## 27 - Split Pea Fritters (Beya Kya) - Myanmar

# 28 - Green Curry with Beef (Gaeng Kiaw Wan Neua) - Thailand

Thai food is unique amongst all the foods of South-East Asia. Situated on the crossroads of East to West sea routes, Thai food became infused with Persian and Arabian elements as well as having influences from Indian and Chinese cuisines. Thai food is readily identifiable from others, incorporating as it does, all the 5 tastes: sweet, sour, bitter, salty, and spicy. Thai people took the foreign influences and created a style of cooking of their own.

This dish is probably one of the better-known recipes from Thailand.

## What you need

400 g beef
1 tbs groundnut oil
3 tbs green curry paste (see below, or use prepared curry paste)
600 ml coconut milk
2 kaffir lime leaves, torn
5-10 small fresh Thai eggplants, quartered
2-3 fresh red spur chillies, sliced diagonally
generous handful sweet basil leaf (optional)
1½ tbs fish sauce
1½ tsp palm sugar
Sweet basil leaves and red chilli slices for garnish

## What to do

Slice the beef into pieces, about 1 cm thick.

Heat oil in a wok over a medium heat then sauté the green curry paste until fragrant. Reduce the heat, gradually add 350 ml of the coconut milk a little at a time, stir until a film of green oil surfaces.

Add the beef and kaffir lime leaves, continue cooking for 3 minutes or until the beef is cooked through. Transfer to a large pan then place over medium heat and cook until boiling. Add the remaining coconut milk, season with palm sugar and fish sauce. When the mixture returns to a boil add the eggplants. Cook until the eggplants are done, sprinkle sweet basil leaves and red chillies over, then turn off the heat.

Arrange on a serving dish and garnish with sweet basil leaves and red chillies before serving.

## Thai Green Chilli Paste

## What you need

15 large fresh green hot chillies
3 shallots, sliced
9 cloves garlic
1 tsp finely sliced fresh galangal
1 tbs sliced fresh lemon grass (lower part only)
½ tsp finely sliced kaffir lime rind (green part only, the white is bitter)
1 tsp chopped coriander root
5 white peppercorns
1 tbs roasted coriander seeds
1 tsp roasted cumin seeds
1 tsp sea salt
1 tsp shrimp paste

# 28 - Green Curry with Beef (Gaeng Kiaw Wan Neua) - Thailand

**What to do**

Combine the coriander seeds, cumin and peppercorn in spice grinder and set aside.
In a blender, combine the remaining ingredients except the shrimp paste. When mixed well.
add the cumin mixture and shrimp paste, blend well.
(A mortar and pestle can be used for both these processes if you prefer)

**Cook's tip:**

For a beautiful green colour paste, combine 4 dark green Jalapeño peppers with 15 fresh hot Thai chilli peppers.

# 29 - Amok Trei - Cambodia

Cambodian cuisine was all but wiped out under Pol Pot and the Khmer Rouge. All cookery books, which the Khmer Rouge considered to be bourgeois, were destroyed. City populations were forced into the countryside at gunpoint to work in the fields to produce food they were not allowed to eat; instead being given a meagre allowance of 180 g of rice which had to last for two days. An estimated two million people were killed to create an agrarian utopian state of peasant farmers.
Pol Pot was overthrown in 1979 but continued to fight the Cambodian government for the next 17 years.
Only in recent years have traditional Cambodian dishes started to be seen once again in the country, surviving only because of the memories and determination of some of the people to retain the history of their own cuisine.
Cambodia lies on the mighty Mekong river, which along with the Tonle Sap and Bassac rivers and Tonle Sap Lake, provides Cambodia with an abundance of freshwater fish.
In this recipe, any white fish can be used; in this case, I used Sea Bass.

## What you need

1 garlic clove, chopped
1 red onion, chopped
5 cm fresh root galangal, chopped or ½ tsp ground galangal
2 tbs chopped lemon grass or 2 tsp ground lemon grass
½ tsp ground turmeric
1 tsp paprika
2 tbs fish sauce
1 tbs sugar
½ tsp salt
1 x 400 g tin coconut milk
450 g white fish fillets
4-8 banana leaves

## What to do

Place the garlic, onion, galangal, lemon grass, turmeric, paprika, fish sauce and sugar in a blender. Process until all ingredients are well blended then add the coconut milk and blend again.
Transfer the coconut mixture to a saucepan and bring to simmering point, whilst stirring continuously. Continue to cook gently for about 10 minutes until thickened.
Gently heat the banana leaves, either on a barbeque, or by steaming to make them pliable. Cut into pieces about 20 cm square.
Place the fish fillets in a bowl, season with a little salt, then pour half the hot coconut sauce over the fish and mix well. Set the remaining sauce aside.
Divide the fish mixture into the same number of portions as you have banana squares. Place the mixture in the centre of each leaf and fold the edges over to form secure parcels.
Steam the parcels for 1 hour.
5 minutes before the end of the cooking time, gently reheat the remaining sauce.
Make a small opening along the centre of each parcel and spoon the remaining coconut sauce into the opening. Serve immediately with rice of your choice.

**Note:** Whilst banana leaves are edible, it isn't recommended to eat them.

## 29 - Amok Trei - Cambodia

# 30 - Green Papaya Salad (Tam Mak Hoong or Tam Som) - Laos

The food in Laos has many regional variations depending on the fresh local foods available in that area. Sticky rice is common to all regions and is a present at almost every meal. The Lao people consume more of this rice than any other country and over three-quarters of the rice grown in Laos is the glutinous variety.

Fresh vegetables are common, and the meat and fish almost always grilled, so the Lao diet is high in vitamins and low in fat, making it healthy.

Lao people were originally from China and brought their cooking methods and styles with them. Traditional Lao cuisine has inevitably been influenced by neighbouring countries, and even the Europeans in the form of the French. Baguettes, especially in the capital Vientiane, a throw-back to the days of French Indochina, and Pho Bo from Vietnam, both feature prominently in Lao cooking. However, the influence has not been all one way. Thai, and to a lesser extent, Cambodian recipes have been strongly influenced by the Lao people as they migrated into the neighbouring regions.

This recipe is easy to make, requiring no cooking and little preparation. You may be more familiar with the Thai version which is known as som tam, rather than the Lao way of saying it, tam som or tam mak hoong.

## What you need

350 g green papaya
125 g green or string beans
4 medium red and green serrano chillies (to taste)
2 large cloves garlic
6 cherry tomatoes, halved
2 tbs small dried shrimps
cabbage and/or iceberg lettuce leaves

### For the dressing

5 tbs lime juice
3 tbs fish sauce **(see Cook's tip)**
3 tbs sugar
4 tbs finely ground dried shrimps
Combine the dressing ingredients in a small bowl and set aside.

## What to do

Shred the papaya flesh into thin strips; a julienning slicer works well. Cut the green beans into 2-3 cm pieces.

Use a mortar and pestle to pound chillies and garlic to coarse texture, then add the papaya and green beans, pound 1-2 minutes longer, mixing with a spoon while pounding. If you don't have a large enough mortar and pestle, work in small batches, Add the tomatoes and pound until they are broken but not completely pulped. Add the dried shrimps and dressing; mix well. Serve with cabbage and lettuce leaves and steamed sticky rice.

This recipe goes well with barbequed meats.

## Cook's tip:

Lao fish sauce (Padaek, sometimes Padek, Lao bagoong) is not like the Thai fish sauce you have probably seen in the supermarkets. Lao fish sauce is produced by fermenting the fish, often contains fish pieces in the jar and is cloudy in appearance. A good substitute is anchovy paste, but the salad will not have quite the same depth of flavour as with padek. Be aware though, padek has a very strong smell and will easily fill a room.

# 30 - Green Papaya Salad (Tam Mak Hoong or Tam Som) - Laos

# 31 - Beef Soup (Pho Bo) - Vietnam

I must confess from the outset; I adore Vietnamese cooking. My first proper taste of what Vietnam has to offer was the street food of the capital, Hanoi. The only way I can describe some of the food is, 'fireworks for the mouth.' Never have I tasted anything before that created such a riot of flavours on the taste buds.

One of the distinctive dishes of Vietnam, which has also been adopted by its neighbours, is pho bo (beef soup), pronounced fuh baa. Served all over Vietnam, this dish is a classic example of how to combine ingredients to produce flavours that are far more than the sum of its parts.

I was lucky enough to attend a one-day cooking class at the Red Bridge Restaurant and Cooking School in Hoi-An, in the central region of Vietnam. Head Chef, Nguyen Thanh, gave up some of his secrets for cooking an excellent pho bo, and I have picked up a couple more since then to add to those from Thanh.

What you see here is a combination of recipes to bring you a pho bo that is more to the style of North Vietnam, using the wider noodle as a base for this delicious dish.

## What you need

### For the broth

2 medium yellow onions
10 cm piece ginger (about 120 g)
2.5 kg beef soup bones (marrow and knuckle bones)
5 star anise
6 whole cloves
8 cm cinnamon stick
500 g piece of beef (cheaper cut), cut into 5x10 cm pieces (trimmed weight)
1½ tbs salt
4 tbs fish sauce (nuoc mam)
30 g yellow rock sugar

### For the pickle

230 ml white vinegar
½ tsp salt
1 tsp sugar
3 cloves garlic - peeled
3 shallots - peeled
1 red chilli
1 green chilli

### For the herbs

Asian basil - also known as Vietnamese mint
saw tooth coriander
Vietnamese celery
1 lime

### For the bowls

About 400 g banh pho noodles (If using dried, prepare according to the packet).
6-8 spring onions, chopped
200 g bean sprouts
300 g fillet of beef - very finely sliced.

## What to do

### For the broth

Char the onion, ginger and bones, preferably on a barbeque for about 15 minutes, turning frequently (this removes some of the fat from the bones and adds flavour to the onion and ginger). Under warm water, remove charred onion skin; trim and discard blackened parts of root or stem ends. Use sharp knife to remove skin from the ginger. Set aside.

Place the bones in stockpot (minimum 12 litre capacity) and cover with cold water. Bring to the boil and boil vigorously for around 30 minutes. Pour the contents of a pan into a large colander. Rinse the bones with warm water and clean the stockpot to remove any residue. Return the bones to pan.

Add 12 litres of water to the pot and bring to boil, then lower to a simmer. Skim off any scum from the surface. Add the remaining broth ingredients and cook, uncovered, for 1 hour then remove the boneless meat; reserve for another dish. Simmer the broth for another 3 hours

# 31 - Beef Soup (Pho Bo) - Vietnam

Strain the broth through a sieve, discarding the solids. (If you are preparing the broth the night before, cool in a refrigerator overnight to make it easier to remove any excess fat before reheating, otherwise skim off as much as desired with a ladle). Adjust the flavour to taste with additional salt, fish sauce and yellow rock sugar.

### For the pickle (Prepare while the stock is cooking)

Put the vinegar in a bowl and add the salt and sugar. Coarsely chop the remaining ingredients and add to the bowl.

### For the herbs

Coarsely chop the Asian basil, saw tooth coriander and Vietnamese celery. Cut the lime into wedges. Arrange in a bowl.
Blanch the noodles, spring onions and beansprouts. Keep the noodles warm in a serving dish. Place the spring onions and beansprouts in separate bowls.

## To serve

Place some of the noodles and raw meat into individual bowls. Pour the hot broth evenly over the meat to cook it. Add beansprouts, spring onions, herbs and pickle to taste.

# 32 - Banh Mi - Vietnam

Two strong indications of past influences on a country are the architecture and food.

The French first had contact with the area we now know as Vietnam, as far back as the 17th century, but it wasn't until the 19th century that they became heavily involved in the region and ultimately formed French Indochina, later to be known as the Indochinese Union, followed by Indochinese Federation. In 1954 the country ceased to be under French control and became the Democratic Republic of Vietnam in the north and the State of Vietnam in the south. The country became unified in 1976.

Even to this day, the French influence can be seen in the architecture; wide boulevards sweep through Ho Chi Minh City, and shuttered windows are a typical feature.

The cuisine has also retained some of this influence, no more so than in a dish that is eaten throughout the country, Banh Mi.

John Montagu, 4th Earl of Sandwich, habitually sent for cold meat in between two slices of bread, so that he wouldn't have to break away from the gambling tables to eat. This we all know now as the sandwich. Banh mi is a very Vietnamese version, the strong French influence showing in the choice of bread, the baguette.

## What you need (makes 1 sandwich)

1 petit baguette or a 7-inch section cut from a regular length baguette (crispy crust)
real mayonnaise (whole egg)
soy sauce
your choice of meat or tofu, sliced (room temperature)
4 thin seeded cucumber strips, pickling or English, if available
3 sprigs coriander, roughly chopped
4 thin Jalapeño pepper slices
do chua (white radish and carrot pickle). **(see Cook's tip)**

## What to do

Cut the bread in half, lengthwise. Hollow out the insides, making a trough in both halves. Discard the removed bread or save for another use, e.g. breadcrumbs. If necessary, crisp the bread in an oven preheated to 160°C, and then allow to cool for a minute before filling.

Spread the insides with a generous portion of mayonnaise and drizzle in the soy sauce. On the bottom portion of bread, layer in the remaining ingredients. Close the sandwich, cut in half if required.

## Cook's tip:

Do chua is easy to make as follows;

## What you need

2 medium carrots, peeled and cut into thick matchsticks
500 g white radish* (also known as daikon or mooli), peeled and cut into thick matchsticks
1 tsp salt
2 tsp sugar
100 g sugar
300 ml distilled white vinegar
240 ml water

## What to do

Place the carrot and radish in a bowl. Sprinkle with the salt and 2 tsp sugar. Use your hands to knead the vegetables for about 3 minutes, expelling the water from them. Stop kneading when the

## 32 - Banh Mi - Vietnam

radish is flexible enough to bend the ends to touch and it doesn't break. The vegetables should have lost about ¼ volume. Drain in a colander and rinse under cold running water. Gently press to expel any retained water. Return to the bowl.

In a pan, combine the remaining sugar, vinegar and water. Heat gently, stirring to dissolve the sugar. Allow to cool. Pour over the vegetable mixture, covering completely. Allow the vegetables to marinate for at least 1 hour before using. This can be kept in a refrigerator for up to 4 weeks but keep it in a jar. The smell will fill the refrigerator in no time if left in a dish.

*Use white radish of no more than 5 cm in diameter.

# 33 - Curry Puffs (Karipap Pusing) - Malaysia

Malaysian cuisine has had many influences over the years, and in fact Malaysia is a country made up of many regions each with their own distinctive styles. As we see so many times in the recipes on this journey around the world, spice traders brought many foodstuffs and techniques that wouldn't have been available at the time and the people combined these with their own ways to produce a cuisine that is distinctive from many others in the far-east.

If you have plenty of time on your hands and are happy to prepare two different types of pastry, there is no reason why you can't do so, but never feel obliged to make pastry from scratch. For this recipe, I chose to use ready-made pastry as it saves considerable time in the kitchen. Traditional curry puffs only have potatoes as a filling, but as with all recipes, feel free to make your own additions to suit your tastes.

## What you need

2 tbs vegetable oil
1 large brown onion, roughly chopped
2 cloves garlic, finely chopped
2-3 tbs curry powder
250 g chicken breast* or chuck steak* diced into small cubes (*optional)
3 large potatoes, peeled, diced into small cubes
½ tsp sugar, or to taste
½ tsp salt, or to taste

## What to do

### For the filling

Heat the oil in a medium frying pan over medium heat.
Sauté the onion and garlic until soft and golden. Add the curry powder, mixing well with the onions and cook for a few seconds until toasted and fragrant.
Add the chicken or steak (if using) and stir-fry until cooked, then add remaining ingredients, stir-frying until the potatoes are tender.
Season to taste. Allow the mixture to cool in a refrigerator before filling the pastry.

### For the pastry

Roll out a sheet of puff pastry, and one of shortcrust pastry into long rectangles approximately 10 cm wide. Lay the shortcrust pastry on top of the puff pastry and roll up like a Swiss roll. Slice the roll into discs approximately 1 cm thick. Roll each disc out to form a circle. You should have approximately 20 discs depending on how much pastry you used.

Place 1-2 heaped tbs of the filling in the centre of each disc, then fold the disc in half, crimping the edges together to seal the filling into the pastry. Traditionally the edges are formed into a rope pattern, similar to the Mongolian Kuushuur, but don't worry if you can't get it to look right, as long as the edge is sealed; as you can see, my pastry crimping skills are severely lacking.

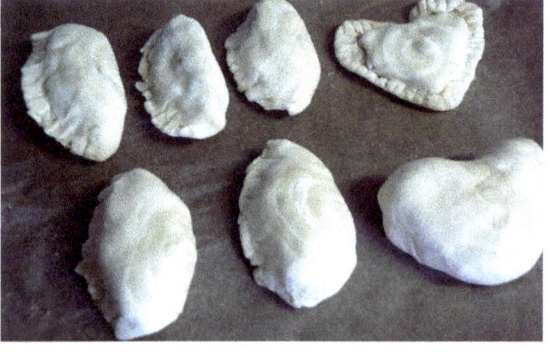

Sealing can be aided by brushing a little egg onto the edges of the pastry before crimping.
As a bit of fun for Valentine's Day, when I first made this dish, I cut some into a heart shape, the principle of sealing being the same.

# 33 - Curry Puffs (Karipap Pusing) - Malaysia

Place the curry puffs on a tray in the fridge until ready to cook.
There are two ways the curry puffs can be cooked, either deep fried or in the oven.

**To fry**

Heat oil in a wok or a deep fat fryer on a medium-high heat. To test the temperature, drop a small piece of leftover pastry into the oil, it should turn golden in 15-20 seconds. Fry 4 curry puffs at a time until the pastry is a beautiful deep golden colour. Drain in a kitchen paper lined colander.

**To oven bake**

Brush the curry puffs with an egg wash (1 egg whisked with 1 tbs of milk). Place on a baking tray and bake at 180°C for about 25-30 minutes until a deep golden colour.
Take care if using a different oven to the one you are used to, otherwise you will burn some like I did (see the photograph!)
Serve hot or at room temperature.

# 34 - Beef Rendang - Indonesia

Along with Vietnamese food, Indonesian cuisine is one of the most vibrant in the world; full of colours and intense flavours. Over 6,000 of the 18,000 islands that form Indonesia are populated and there are over 300 ethnic groups who call Indonesia their home. This leads to many regional variations in cooking, often based upon local culture as well as foreign influences. We could write an entire series on Indonesia alone, with well over 5,000 traditional recipes. Indonesian cuisine often includes rice, noodle and soup dishes and as with many of the Far Eastern cuisines, food can range from simple dishes sold by street vendors to more complex and expensive dishes sold in restaurants.

This recipe is primarily for beef, but lamb or goat are good alternatives and lend themselves well to this dish.

## What you need

### For the beef

1 kg beef cut into cubes
4 tbs oil
1 cinnamon stick
3 cloves
3 star anise
3 cardamom pods
1 stalk lemongrass (cut into 10 cm length and pounded)
400 ml coconut cream
2 tsp tamarind paste
6 kaffir lime leaves (finely sliced)
6 tbs toasted coconut (kerisik)
1 tbs palm sugar or to taste
salt to taste

### For the spice paste

5 shallots
2.5 cm galangal
3 stalks lemongrass (white part only)
5 cloves garlic
2.5 cm ginger
3 fresh chillies deseeded and chopped, or 6 dried chillies, deseeded and chopped.
2 tbs of ground nut oil

## What to do

Add the spice paste ingredients to a food processor and blend until fine.
Heat the oil in a large saucepan, add the spice paste, cinnamon, cloves, star anise, and cardamom; stir-fry until aromatic.
Add the beef and the pounded lemongrass and stir for 1 minute. Add the coconut milk and tamarind. Simmer on medium heat, stirring frequently until the meat is almost cooked.
Add the kaffir lime leaves, toasted coconut, palm sugar and salt, blend well with the meat.
Lower the heat and cover the pan with a lid. Simmer for 1 - 1½ hours or until the meat is tender and the liquid has dried up. Drain excess oil as necessary.
Serve with steamed rice.

# 34 - Beef Rendang - Indonesia

**Cook's tip:**

To prepare the toasted coconut (kerisik), add grated coconut to a dry wok or frying pan and stir continuously until the coconut turns golden brown. Take care as it only takes a few seconds to go from golden brown to dark brown.

# 35 - Banana Pancakes - Papua New Guinea

Archaeological evidence suggests that humans settled in Papua New Guinea approximately 35,000 years ago.

In more recent times, various parts of the country have come under the jurisdiction of the Germans, British, Dutch and Australians. Despite this, there appears to have been little influence on the traditional cuisine for many of the population.

Perhaps this is caused by the relative inaccessibility of the country and many people having little contact with outsiders; the Central Highlands region wasn't even mapped until the nineteen-thirties. In past recipes, we have seen how the spice traders influenced the cooking of the indigenous population, but the story here is different with little spice being used in the Papuan cuisine. It is a different in the cities, where the food has become more westernised.

For most of the people, the diet is largely vegetarian and relies heavily on taro roots, sweet potatoes and sago. An abundance of fruits supplement the diet; banana, coconut, guava, mango, papaya, pineapple, and watermelon often accompany meals. Coastal villages add fish, crab and crayfish to the table. Meat is usually cooked on special occasions.

For this recipe, I have chosen a simple dessert; banana pancakes.

## What you need

### For the pancake

270 g self-raising flour
¼ tsp baking powder
240 ml milk
2 tbs honey
45 g butter, melted
2-3 very ripe bananas, mashed

### For the topping

1-2 bananas, sliced
honey

## What to do

Sift the flour and baking powder into a mixing bowl. Make a well in the middle. Combine the remaining ingredients, add to the flour and beat until lump free. Add flour or milk as necessary to get a thick consistency. Too thin and you will only be able to make crêpes.

Melt a little extra butter in a large frying or crêpe pan. Once the pan is hot, spoon in desired amount of mixture **(see Cook's tips)**

As soon as bubbles start to form in the batter, flip over the pancake and cook the other side. Top with sliced bananas and drizzle with honey.

You can use any fresh fruit, add a squeeze of lemon/lime and a sprinkle of sugar.

## Cook's tips:

The type of pancake you make is entirely up to you. Thin ones like French crêpes or thick ones like American, is a matter of personal choice. Use a thinner batter to make crêpes.

To form a perfectly round American style pancake, pour the batter into an egg ring in the pan. Remove the ring before you flip the pancake.

# 36 - Chilli Taiyo and Noodles - Solomon Islands

Just how and when the Solomon Islands were first settled remains unclear, but it is thought there have been people on the islands for some 25,000-3,0000 years. The early settlers were probably Papuan with Austronesian speakers arriving some 6,000 years ago followed sometime later by the Polynesians and Lapita people.

The first Europeans arrived in the 16$^{th}$ century when the Spaniard Álvaro de Mendaña visited from Peru. It wasn't until the 19$^{th}$ century the Europeans returned in the shape of the British and Germans, but full responsibility for the Islands was assumed later by the British when they became a protectorate of the British Crown. During that time, other nationalities were introduced to work on the coconut plantations and with them they brought spices and cooking techniques.

The islands saw some of the fiercest fighting in the Pacific theatre during WWII, especially around Guadalcanal. In 1978, the Solomon Islands became a sovereign nation.

It is not surprising that living on a collection of almost 1,000 islands, the Solomon Islanders rely heavily on fish in their cuisine and at one time, exported tuna which was canned on one of the 6 main islands.

## What you need

2 tuna steaks or fillets, seasoned **(see Cook's tips)**
300 g noodles
1 onion, chopped
1 green chilli, chopped **(see Cook's tips)**
3 tbs soy sauce
3 spring onions, chopped
2 tbs olive oil

## What to do

Heat 1 tbs of the olive oil in a saucepan. Fry the onion and chilli until softened.
Add the noodles and 100 ml water, cover and steam for about 10 minutes before adding the soy sauce and spring onions. Cook for a further 3 minutes.
Use the remaining olive oil to fry the tuna steaks for a few minutes on each side to taste.
Divide the noodles into portions and top with a tuna portion.

## Cook's tips:

Either tuna steaks or fillets are suitable for this dish, but canned tuna can be used if wished.

Use whatever chillies suit your palate.

# 36 - Chilli Taiyo and Noodles - Solomon Islands

# 37 - Mango Chutney - Vanuatu

The Republic of Vanuatu is a Pacific island nation in the South Pacific Ocean. The islands are of volcanic origin and are located to the southeast of the Solomon Islands, and west of Fiji.
Vanuatu was first inhabited by Melanesian people some 2,500 years ago. The first Europeans to visit the islands were in a Spanish expedition led by Portuguese navigator Fernandes de Queirós, who arrived in the 17th century. In the early 20th century the archipelago came under joint administration by the British and French, and in 1980 the islands gained their independence when the Republic of Vanuatu was founded.
Prior to contact with the western world, the islanders would principally use bananas, coconuts, greens, pigs, fowl, seafood, sugarcane, taro, tropical nuts, and yams in their cooking. With the advent of growing crops for commercial gain, particularly by European plantation owners, other foods such as, beans, cabbage, carrots, corn, mango, manioc, papaya, peppers, plantain, pumpkin and sweet potato, were added to the diet. Generally, rural people produce most of what they eat, supplementing the diet with luxury foods (rice and tinned fish) purchased in stores.
This recipe is relatively easy to make, but very tasty.

## What you need

3 half-ripe mangoes
2 tbs oil
½ tsp hot chilli powder
¼ tsp cumin
1 clove garlic, finely chopped
1 piece root ginger, about 2.5 cm, peeled and finely chopped
1 tsp salt
1 tbs lemon juice
385 g light brown sugar **(see Cook's tip)**
300 ml cider vinegar

## What to do

Peel and cut the mangoes into thin slices. Only use the soft fruit and not the fibrous parts from around the stones.
Heat the oil in a large saucepan and add the mangoes, chilli powder, cumin, garlic, ginger and salt. Cook gently for 2 minutes, stirring constantly.
Add the lemon juice, sugar and vinegar. Bring to a boil and simmer uncovered for 40-50 minutes, or until the liquid has become syrupy and the mangoes translucent.
In the meantime, sterilise the jars and lids by boiling in a large pan. Ensure the jars remain covered whilst boiling and stand them on a trivet to allow the water to pass all around the jar. Remove from the water and drain.
Whilst the jars are still hot, ladle in the hot chutney, leaving about 5 mm head space.
Release any trapped air in the jars and seal with the lids.
Allow to cool before storing in a refrigerator for up to two months.

## Cook's tip:

The sugar you use will determine the colour of the chutney I used a darker sugar because I like the molasses flavour in my chutney.

## 37 - Mango Chutney - Vanuatu

# 38 - Macadamia Nut Cookies - Australia

The macadamia tree is native to Australia, so it is no surprise the Aboriginal Australians have known about this 'bush tucker' for many centuries. Bush tucker is any food native to Australia and would have been used by the Aboriginal Australians in their diet. The Aborigines had a varied diet including such meats as kangaroo, emu and crocodile. Plant derived foods would include fruits such as quandong, kutjera and finger lime, leafy vegetables such as warrigal greens, and spices including lemon and aniseed myrtles and mountain pepper. Nuts, of course, were also prominent in the diet, the most well-known one being the macadamia.

Probably the most significant modern national holiday for the Aborigines is Australia's national Journey of Healing Day, better known as Sorry Day, stemming from the government's recognition that forcing a European lifestyle upon the Aboriginal people was wrong. Aborigines often use this day to show off some of their best native cuisine. For them, as with many other cultures, food is closely associated with spirituality.

This recipe makes use of the macadamia nut and is easy to make.

## What you need

½ tsp baking soda
325 g icing sugar
310 g all-purpose flour
¼ tsp salt
115 g butter
115 g shortening **(see Cook's tip)**
2 eggs
230 g macadamia nuts, chopped and roasted

## What to do

Preheat the oven to 180°C.
Combine the dry ingredients; baking soda, icing sugar, flour, and salt in a bowl.
In a separate bowl, mix the butter, shortening, and eggs until smooth. For this I used an electric mixer as it makes life a lot easier.
Add the dried mixture to the bowl and mix until all the ingredients are combined. Add the nuts and continue mixing for a few minutes.
Drop heaped tsp of the dough, about 5 cm apart, on an ungreased cookie sheet or baking tray. Don't worry if they stand up like bonsai mountains, they will soon flatten into a regular cookie shape in the oven.
Bake for 10-12 minutes.
Cook in batches until all the dough is used.
Allow to cool on a wire rack.

Makes 3-4 dozen cookies.

## Cook's tip:

For shortening I used beef suet, but vegetable shortening is also suitable.

## 38 - Macadamia Nut Cookies - Australia

# 39 - Sweet and Sour Beef - New Zealand

New Zealand was first populated by the Polynesians, probably in the 13th century. The isolated nature of the islands resulted in these settlers developing their own culture and way of living, which we now know as Māori. The original settlers brought plants with them and developed their own horticulture, combining it with the indigenous plant and animal life for use in their cuisine. In common with other Polynesians, the Māori used earth ovens which in New Zealand are known as hāngi.

In the late 18th century, the Europeans arrived, bringing with them foodstuffs new to the Māori, which they soon adopted. Initial settlers had to rely on local produce to try to recreate some of the food of home; brewing tea using unconventional leaves for instance. As more settlers came to New Zealand, the importation of foodstuffs increased, and regular ingredients became more widely available.

In the 19th and 20th centuries, many other nationalities adopted New Zealand as their home and the cuisine altered again as the methods and ingredients of those nationalities were adopted.

This dish is an example of this; sweet and sour being traditionally a far-eastern dish, but the method of cooking is more western.

## What you need

300 g chuck steak or similar, cubed
1 red onion
1 carrot
1 green pepper
1 parsnip
340 g can pineapple chunks
400 g can chopped tomatoes
1 tbs soy sauce
1 tbs flour **(see Cook's tip)**
150 g peas, cooked

## What to do

Dice the carrot, green pepper and parsnip into 2 cm pieces. Cut the red onion into slices. Brown the steak in a heavy based frying pan then transfer to a slow cooker*. Add the red onion to pan with the beef juices and cook until soft. Add the cooked onion to the meat along with the carrot, pepper, parsnip, pineapple, tomatoes and soy sauce. Put on the lid and cook on high for 1 hour, then turn to low and cook a further 3-4 hours. Season to taste.
Add the peas before serving.
Goes well with unpeeled, scrubbed new potatoes and steamed broccoli.

## Cook's tip:

If the liquid requires thickening, mix a heaped tbs of all-purpose flour with a small amount of water, make into a smooth paste. Add to meat as needed when cooked then cook on high for a further 15 minutes.

### *Cooking without a slow cooker

Preheat the oven to 100°C. Prepare everything as for a slow cooker then transfer all the ingredients to a heavy based saucepan. Add 100-200 ml of water and cook on a high heat for 10 minutes. Stir regularly. Transfer to a heavy casserole dish or Dutch Oven, cover and place in the oven for 2-3 hours. Stir frequently to avoid sticking. Check all ingredients are cooked thoroughly and extend cooking time if necessary.

# 39 - Sweet and Sour Beef - New Zealand

# 40 - Sweet Potato and Pineapple Bake - Fiji

Like the Solomon Islanders, the indigenous Fijians are descended from the Lapita peoples. This seafaring group arrived from eastern Indonesia and the Philippines around 4,000 years ago. Later, Melanesians from the west and Polynesians from the east, also descendants of the Lapita, came to the islands to settle.

During the 19$^{th}$ century, the Europeans arrived; planters and traders attempted to set up a colony on the model of those of Australia and New Zealand.

Sugarcane plantations were suggested by the British as a means by which the islands could gain economic self-sufficiency. To preserve the traditional way of life of the Fijians, the first Indian indentured labourers were brought to the islands in 1879 to work on the plantations. Conditions for these workers were harsh, but many chose to remain after their contracts ended because of the depressed economic situation in India.

Fijian cuisine adopted methods and ingredients from these cultures, but even to this day, Fijian and Indo-Fijian dishes differ. However, the Fijians have adopted chilli peppers, unleavened bread, rice, vegetables, curries, and tea, and the Indo-Fijians have accepted taro and cassava as part of their diet.

This recipe uses a traditional staple, sweet potato, and mixes it with other foods that would be readily available to the Fijians.

## What you need

2 medium sweet potatoes, baked, peeled and cut into 10 mm thick slices
1 fresh pineapple, peeled, cored and cut into 5 mm thick slices
30 g freshly grated coconut
25 g spring onions, chopped
240 ml cheese sauce (see below)
sea salt and fresh ground pepper to taste

## What to do

Preheat the oven to 180°C. Layer a lightly buttered casserole or pie dish with the sweet potato, followed by the pineapple, coconut and finally the green onions. Season each completed layer with the sea salt and freshly ground pepper. Prepare the cheese sauce as described below, then pour the sauce over the top. Bake for 30 minutes. Serve hot.

### For the cheese sauce

## What you need

85 g butter
50 g flour
600 ml light cream
2 tsp dry mustard
200 g cheddar cheese, grated

## What to do

Combine flour and butter in heavy pan over medium heat. Cook for 2 minutes, until flour starts to brown. Slowly stir in the cream. Stir constantly until the desired consistency is achieved **(see Cook's tip)**, then add the cheese, mustard; salt and pepper to taste. Stir until cheese is melted, remove from heat and use immediately.

## Cook's tip:

If the sauce is too thick, add some milk to the pan; if too thin, add some more flour mixed with a small amount of water.

## 40 - Sweet Potato and Pineapple Bake - Fiji

# 41 - Chop Suey (Sapa Sui) - Samoa

The History of Samoa is complex. Thought to have been first settled some 3,500 years ago, Samoa remained relatively untouched until the early 18th century. Since then, many countries have been involved in the politics and government of these South Pacific Islands. Whilst at first it appears Samoan cuisine is quite simple, with many variations around one ingredient, it is in fact adaptable and versatile, depending on what produce is available according to season and locality.

The Europeans and Chinese have been major influences on the cuisine. Traditional dishes such as umu (oven-pit-baked food), sapa sui (chop suey, from the late 19th century contact with the United States), and puligi (a steamed pudding) have not changed much over the last few decades. Others have not done so well, such as suamasi (cracker soup), which is no longer eaten.

## What you need

250 g bean vermicelli (also known as cellophane, glass noodles, Chinese vermicelli)
2 tbs oil
1 large onion, diced
2-4 garlic cloves, crushed
1 tbs grated ginger
500 g of chopped meat, beef or chicken **(see Cook's tips)**
2 tbs soy sauce
460 ml water
100 ml soy sauce
2 tbs ketchup manis
1 small pak choi, chopped
2 carrots, thinly sliced, diagonally
2 sticks celery, chopped
60 g green beans, sliced diagonally
1 tsp vegetable, chicken or beef stock powder

## What to do

In a large pan or wok, fry the onion, garlic and ginger over a medium-high heat until the onion is translucent. Add the meat and stir-fry until just seared.

Add the soy sauce and water (the water should almost cover the meat). Let simmer over a medium heat while the noodles are prepared as per the instructions on the pack (about 5 minutes).

Add to the pan the noodles plus 200 ml of the noodle cooking water and the remaining ingredients. At this stage, it will look more like a soup.

Stir and let simmer over a medium heat for 10-15 minutes until the water has been absorbed. Serve with steamed rice.

## Cook's tips:

Any vegetables can be used to suit your own tastes. Works well with white cabbage, broccoli and peas to name a few.

Minced meat can be used if desired. Reduce the quantity to 300 g.

# 41 - Chop Suey (Sapa Sui) - Samoa

# 42 - Marinated Fresh Fish (Poisson Cru) - Tahiti

We have already seen evidence of the migration of the peoples of South-East Asia, towards the east, through the Solomon Islands, Vanuatu, Fiji and Samoa.
This exodus didn't reach Tahiti until somewhere between 500-1,000 years after the first settlers arrived in Samoa.
For many centuries, the people of this group of islands, we now know as French Polynesia, remained isolated from outside influences. As with the other islands, the cuisine became a product of what was available locally. Fish and fruit dominated, along with crops such as sweet potato.
It wasn't until the mid $18^{th}$ century, the Europeans arrived in Tahiti, with both the British and the French claiming sovereignty.
Although the Europeans and other nations have influenced the cuisine, traditional recipes and methods remain in daily use to this day.
One of the most famous of the traditional dishes from Tahiti is Poisson Cru, literally translating as 'raw fish.'
This recipe uses acid from the limes to cook the fish. The scientific process by which meat and fish are cooked by acids (denaturation), is the same as that which occurs in an oven, although the texture is considerably different when things are cooked by this method.

## What you need

500 g fresh tuna
2 carrots
2 tomatoes
8 limes
3 small green onions (spring onions)
1 clove garlic, crushed
1 small cucumber
cream of one grated coconut **(see Cook's tip)**
salt and pepper to taste

## What to do

Cut the tuna into small cubes (around 1½cm square) and rinse with salted water. Add enough salted water to cover the tuna cubes and add the crushed garlic. Allow to soak for ½ hour in the refrigerator.
Grate coarsely or chop the vegetables.
Drain the tuna, then cover with the juice of the limes, allowing the fish to 'cook' for about 5 minutes in the lime juice. Drain and discard the lime juice. Add the vegetables and the coconut cream and mix well. Add salt and pepper to taste. Serve chilled.
Makes an excellent starter.

## Cook's tip:

To make coconut cream, boil 1 part water with 4 parts shredded coconut. Allow to cool then refrigerate before using.

## 42 - Marinated Fresh Fish (Poisson Cru) -Tahiti

# 43 - Po'e - Easter Island

When we think of Easter Island, also known as Rapa Nui, we think of the large stone statues, called moai. Many people believe these were erected to honour clan chiefs, ancestors or important personages, but as the inhabitants of the island have no written history we cannot be certain. Often, people believe that just the heads are present, but in fact it has been shown that the statues are complete, and the rest of the body is present beneath the head under the ground.

One of the most isolated islands in the world, Easter Island is thought to have first become inhabited by the Polynesians, some 2,800 years ago. There are some theories that the people of Polynesia originated in South America, one which has some support from the fact that the sweet potato is native to South America and is present throughout Polynesia.

As would be expected from an island nation, the cuisine relies heavily on local produce, especially seafood and easily grown crops.

The dish has few ingredients and is easy to make.

Po'e is used to accompany many meals including the curanto* and in some cases ceviche**. It is a type of cake, made from pumpkin, flour, and plantain or banana, that is sweet and quite spongy.

* Curanto consists of seafood, meat, potatoes and vegetables and is traditionally prepared in a hole in the ground.
**Ceviche is a raw fish dish 'cooked' in citrus juice, such as the Poisson Cru from Tahiti.

## What you need

2 large ripe bananas, mashed
250 g grated pumpkin
240 g flour
125 ml vegetable oil
100 g grated coconut
125 g cane sugar

## What to do

Preheat oven to 180°C.

Mash the banana in a bowl. Add the grated pumpkin and gradually add half of the flour, mixing well. Add the oil, sugar, grated coconut and remaining flour, combine well. The mixture should have the consistency of a puree and be fairly runny.

Butter a baking or loaf tin then pour in the mixture. It should fill the tin to about ¾ full. Bake for 45 minutes to an hour, or until pudding is firm and a skewer inserted, comes out clean. Remove from the oven and allow to cool on a rack.

Cover with plastic cling wrap and chill in refrigerator.

Goes exceptionally well with coconut ice-cream.

## 43 - Po'e - Easter Island

# 44 - Cazuela de Vaca - Chile

South America is almost certainly where the humble potato originated.
This vast continent has a variety of landscapes; mountains, high plains, rainforest, pampas, pastoral lands and coastal regions to name but a few. Temperatures range from the cold and snowy Tierra del Fuego in the south, to the tropical islands off the coast of Venezuela in the north. As would be expected, ingredients vary tremendously; fish, seafood and tropical fruits from warmer coastal areas; meat, cereals and root crops from some of the higher and colder regions.
Chile is a long and narrow country on the west coast of the continent. It stretches some 4,300 km north to south but boasts a mere 350km at its widest point; bordered entirely by the Pacific Ocean to the west and the Andes to the east.
This dish is a traditional stew, which as always, you can make according to the recipe, or add your own variations.

## What you need

650 g beef (brisket, silverside or similar) cut into six large chunks
1 litre beef broth (stock pots or cubes are fine, but for the best results use beef bones and make your own).
470 ml water
40 g polenta (coarse or fine)
8 red potatoes, cut in half
1 onion, quartered
650 g slice of pumpkin, cut into six pieces
2 ears corn, cut into thirds
1 carrot, cut into 1 cm slices
1 small red bell pepper, seeded and cut into 2.5 cm square pieces
1 stick celery, cut into chunks
1 leek, split in half, then cut into 1 cm pieces
1 tsp fresh oregano, finely chopped
¼ tsp mild paprika
salt and pepper to taste
1 small bunch coriander leaves, coarsely chopped

## What to do

Lightly brown the beef in a frying pan, then place into a large saucepan. Add the broth and water. Bring to a boil over high heat, reduce the heat and cover the pan. Simmer until tender; about 1-1½ hours.
Add the polenta, potatoes and onion. Simmer the covered pan for a further 15 minutes. Add the pumpkin to the stew along with the corn, carrot, bell pepper, celery, and leek; simmer until the vegetables are tender, adding more water if needed to barely cover. Stir in the oregano and paprika during the last 5 minutes.
Season to taste.
Ladle into serving bowls, and sprinkle with chopped coriander.

## 44 - Cazuela de Vaca - Chile

# 45 - Chimichurri Bread - Argentina

Go to any Argentinian restaurant and you are almost guaranteed to find Chimichurri sauce. The origins of the name of this condiment are somewhat confused; some say it is a corruption of the name Jimmy McCurry, others believe it to come from overhearing a group of Europeans saying, 'give me the curry' However the sauce got its name, it almost certainly originated in Argentina and Uruguay.

The ingredients for the sauce centre around parsley, pepper, olive oil and garlic; the bread recipe shares the same ingredients making it as equally delicious. The inclusion of cayenne pepper gives it just enough bite on the palate. Beef goes particularly well with this bread and it makes excellent sandwiches or use as an accompaniment for a stew.

## What you need

235 ml water
1½ tbs white wine vinegar (cider vinegar can be substituted)
4 tbs olive oil
⅛ tsp cayenne pepper
¾ tsp dried oregano
2 cloves garlic, minced
3 tbs chopped onion
3 tbs fresh parsley, chopped
1½ tsp salt
1 tbs white sugar
3 tbs wheat bran (oat bran or whole meal flour can be substituted)
360 g bread flour
2 tsp active dry yeast

## What to do

### Bread machine

Place ingredients in the pan of the bread machine in the order recommended by the manufacturer. Select Basic or White Cycle; press Start.

### Traditional

Combine the cayenne pepper, oregano, garlic, onion, parsley, sugar and wheat bran in a large bowl. Stir in the salt. Make a well in the centre. Add the water, vinegar and olive oil.

Use a wooden spoon to stir the mixture until the ingredients are well combined, then use your hands to bring the dough together in the bowl. Turn out onto a lightly floured surface. Knead for 10 minutes or until the dough is smooth and elastic.

Brush a large bowl with olive oil. Place the dough in the bowl and cover with a damp tea towel. Set aside in a warm, draught-free place to prove for 45-60 minutes or until the dough has almost doubled in size.

Punch down the centre of the dough. Turn onto a lightly floured surface. Knead for 2 minutes or until the dough is elastic and has returned to its original size.

Place the dough into a well-oiled loaf tin and allow to prove again for another 30-45 minutes or almost doubled in size again.

Bake in a preheated oven at 200°C for 20-25 minutes or until golden brown.

## Cook's tip:

You can make the dough in the bread maker and then bake traditionally in the oven. This was the method I chose, but don't get distracted like I did, or you will have bread that is much darker than you expected. The Scots call this well-fired and the rest of the world calls it burnt!

## 45 - Chimichurri Bread - Argentina

# 46 - El Postre Chaja - Uruguay

One of the things we see consistently throughout this book is the influence other countries have brought to bear on cuisine around the world; Uruguay is no exception. From the early 16$^{th}$ century, European influences in the form of the Portuguese, and then Spanish settlers, began to shape the cuisine of Uruguay. Later came French, Italian and German with their own methods and recipes. The European influence on this country is so great that in a 2011 census, over 87% of the population laid claim to European origins.

Meat dominates, especially beef which was introduced by the Spaniards, but other meats and fish are still used, as well as a variety of vegetables.

Instead of a meat dish, I have chosen a rich and tasty dessert. It takes a fair amount of work, especially if you don't have an electric whisk, but the results are worth it.

## What you need

### For the sponge

melted butter
4 eggs, at room temperature
165 g caster sugar
60 ml milk
20 g butter
110 g self-raising flour, plus extra to dust
30 g cornflour

### For the meringue

2 egg whites
110 g caster sugar
1 tsp vanilla essence

### For assembly

400 g tin sliced peaches in juice
55 g caster sugar
500 ml thickened cream
1 tsp natural vanilla essence or extract
2 x 20 cm sponge cakes
225 g dulce de leche, warmed slightly (caramelised, sweetened condensed milk)

## What to do

### For the sponge

Preheat the oven to 170°C. Brush 2x20 cm shallow (sandwich) cake tins with some of the melted butter. Line the bases with baking paper; brush the paper with the remaining melted butter. Dust the bases and sides of the tins with a little flour.

Using an electric whisk on medium, whisk the eggs until frothy. Add the sugar a spoonful at a time, whisking well between each addition, until the mixture is very thick and pale (about 8 minutes). Draw a figure eight on the mixture, if it stays on the surface long enough for you to finish drawing, the mixture is ready. If not, whisk for a further minute and then test again.

Heat the milk and butter in a small saucepan over medium heat, until the butter melts. Remove from the heat. Sift the flour and cornflour together over the egg mixture. Immediately pour the warm milk mixture down the side of the bowl - not into the egg mixture directly - and whisk again briefly until the flour mixture is just incorporated (be careful not to overmix).

Divide evenly between the cake tins and gently tap the tins on the worktop to settle. Bake in preheated oven for 18-20 minutes or until a pale golden colour, springs back when lightly touched in the centre, and starts to pull away from the sides of the tins. Remove from the oven and stand for 2 minutes before turning onto a wire rack, top-side up, to cool completely.

The cake, without the meringues on top, will keep in the fridge for up to 3 hours. Stand at room temperature for 30 minutes before serving.

# 46 - El Postre Chaja - Uruguay

**For the meringues**

Preheat the oven to 110°C. Line a large oven tray with non-stick baking paper. Warm the sugar in the oven for about 5 minutes. Place the egg white in the bowl of an electric mixer and start to whisk. Add half the sugar and allow to combine before adding the other half. Continue whisking until the mixture is very thick and glossy and stands in peaks. Spoon into a large piping bag with a plain 1 cm nozzle. Pipe small 'kisses' about 2.5 cm in diameter and 2 cm apart on the lined tray. Bake in preheated oven for 1 hour or until the meringue is crisp and hard to touch, but not coloured. Allow to cool completely in the switched off oven with the door slightly ajar (about 1 hour).

**To assemble**

Drain the peach slices, reserving 100 ml of the juice. Set the peach slices aside. Combine the reserved juice in a small saucepan with the sugar and stir over a low heat until the sugar dissolves. Bring to a simmer and simmer gently for 2 minutes to reduce slightly. Remove from the heat.
Use a mixer or balloon whisk and whisk the cream and vanilla until soft peaks form.
Turn the sponge layers upside down and brush with half the peach syrup. Turn the sponges right way up and brush with the remaining syrup. Place one layer on a serving plate and spread with half the dulce de leche. Spread with one third of the whipped cream. Crumble over about 12 of the meringues and then top with the peach slices (reserving 6 for the top). Cover with the remaining sponge layer. Spread the top with the remaining dulce de leche and then spread the remaining cream over the top and sides. Decorate the top with the remaining meringues and peach slices. Serve immediately.

# 47 - Chicken soup with dumplings (Vori Vori Con Pollo) - Paraguay

Paraguay, sometimes known as the 'Heart of South America' owing to its central location, is a landlocked country lying between Brazil and Bolivia. Although fish is used in the cuisine, only fresh water varieties would have been available to the inhabitants before colonisation and this is reflected in the recipes; most are based on meat, vegetables, cassava and corn (maize).
The inevitable influence from European cuisine has shaped the dishes, particularly when Spanish settlers arrived in the 16th century.
The recipe is for a satisfying soup and is relatively easy to make. The dumplings (vori vori) are not difficult and make this dish very filling. The quantity of black pepper gives the soup quite a bite, so if you like things to be a little milder, reduce the black pepper accordingly.

## What you need

### For the chicken

2 kg whole chicken (corn-fed if you can find it)
1 red pepper, de-seeded, chopped
1 tomato, peeled, chopped
3 garlic cloves, chopped
1 onion, chopped
2 tsp salt
1 tsp black pepper
15 g parsley leaves, coarsely chopped
1 tbs oregano leaves, coarsely chopped, plus extra to serve
1 tbs olive oil

### For the dumplings (vori vori)

160 g cornmeal flour **(see Cook's tip)**
90 g fine semolina
100 g fresh ricotta
1 egg, lightly beaten
2 tsp finely chopped oregano
50 g mozzarella, finely grated

## What to do

### For the chicken

Place the chicken in a large pan with 3 litres of water and bring to a simmer. Cook gently for 50-60 minutes. Skim the surface regularly. Remove the chicken from the stock when the chicken is cooked through and the stock is well flavoured. Once cooled, roughly shred the chicken and set aside.
Mix together the remaining ingredients, except for the olive oil, and set aside.

### For the dumplings

Combine the cornmeal flour and semolina in a bowl. Mix together the ricotta, egg, mozzarella and oregano then add to the flour. Season to taste.
Skim a little of the fat from the surface of the stock, along with 185 ml of the liquid and add just enough to the flour mixture to form a smooth dough. Combine well using your hands adding more stock if necessary, until the dough just comes together. Roll into 1½ cm diameter balls and set aside.
Place a large saucepan over medium-high heat. Add the olive oil and allow to heat. Fry the chopped vegetables in the oil for 5 minutes, stirring continually, until aromatic. Add the chicken stock and bring to the boil. Reduce the heat and simmer for 20 minutes. Add the vori vori balls and cook for 5 minutes.
Return the Chicken to the stock and allow to warm through for a few more minutes.
Ladle soup into bowls and scatter with the extra oregano.

# 47 - Chicken soup with dumplings (Vori Vori Con Pollo) - Paraguay

**Cook's tip:**

Cornmeal flour, also called harina pan and is sometimes sold as polenta. It is not as fine as cornflour.

# 48 - Silpancho - Bolivia

Bolivia, like Paraguay, is entirely landlocked; the country shares borders with Argentina, Paraguay, Brazil, Peru and Chile. While researching for this book, it was not unusual to find a wide range of dishes for the various countries, but this was not the case for Bolivia. Although there were early influences from the Spanish, followed by several nations at later dates, the cuisine does not seem to have matured as much as some of the others in the region; a comment often made on websites was the food is uninspiring and bland. Except for fried guinea pig, most of the dishes rely on staple foods and meats with little or no imagination in the ingredients or methods. So, it came as a surprise this dish was a tasty as it turned out to be.

The combination may not be what we are used to, and it certainly doesn't look that good, but in some strange way, it does work.

### What you need

180 g long-grain rice
470 ml water
3 medium potatoes
1 small green pepper, diced
½ small red onion, diced
1 tomato, diced (I used several cherry tomatoes instead)
2 tsp vinegar
2 tsp vegetable oil
450 g lean minced beef
salt & pepper to taste
100 g breadcrumbs
canola or sunflower oil

### What to do

Place the rice in a pan with the water. Cover and bring to the boil. As soon as boiling, turn off the heat and allow to stand for 15 minutes.

Place the whole potatoes in another pan, bring to the boil and cook for 10 minutes. Once cool enough to touch, cut into 3-4 mm thick slices.

Add salt and pepper to taste to the minced beef and combine with your hands. Divide the minced beef into balls the size of a kiwi fruit.

Sprinkle freshly ground pepper onto a pile of breadcrumbs and then roll the beef in the bread crumbs to give it a light coating.

Pat the ball down flat to create a circle then roll out with a rolling pin over the breadcrumbs, turning frequently to recoat with breadcrumbs until you have created a 'pancake' of beef, about the thickness of a crêpe.

Place the completed 'pancakes' on a plate ready to cook.

Pan sear the 'pancakes' on medium high heat and turn over when the top starts to turn brown.

Stack each finished pancake on a plate and keep warm in the oven.

In the same pan, fry the potato rounds until brown on both sides. Place in the oven to keep warm.

Mix together the chopped tomato, red onion, and green pepper. Cover with the vinegar and oil then combine until well mixed.

Fry the eggs in the same frying pan used for the potatoes and meat.

### To serve

Place a layer of potatoes on a plate, cover with a layer of rice, place a slice of the beef over the top, add the egg and top off with the salad.

## 48 - Silpancho - Bolivia

# 49 - Shrimp Stew (Vatapá) - Brazil

Brazil is the world's 5th largest country. Evidence of human settlement has been established going back 11,000 years. In 1500, the country was claimed by the Portuguese, who established the first settlement in 1532. The country remained relatively stable until the early part of the 19th century, when tension between Portugal and Brazil ultimately resulted in a declaration of independence. Brazil borders almost every country in the South American continent; Ecuador and Chile being the only two exceptions.
Accounting for almost 50% of the continent's land mass, it is only to be expected that such a large nation will have a wealth of variation in the cuisine. Whilst some dishes such as Feijoada, a bean stew of Portuguese origin, have become national favourites, regional dishes have been preserved. Vatapá is found mainly in the north and north-east of the country.

## What you need

200 g dried shrimp
75 g unsalted cashews
60 g unsalted peanuts
150 g day-old French or Italian bread, torn
800 ml unsweetened coconut milk
1 large tomato, roughly chopped
1 medium onion, roughly chopped
2 tbs fresh ginger, peeled and roughly chopped
60 g fresh coriander, plus some for garnish
150 g spring onions, roughly chopped
1 large Jalapeño pepper, cored
150 ml groundnut oil *(see note)
1 tsp turmeric *(see note)
salt and freshly ground black pepper
1 tbs canola oil
450 g large, raw shrimp, cleaned and deveined

## What to do

Clean the dried shrimp by removing the heads and tails with a sharp knife (some dried shrimp is sold this way).
Use a food processor to pulse the dried shrimp until it turns into powder.
Add the cashews and peanuts and continue to process for 2 minutes, until incorporated. Remove from food processor and set aside.
Place the bread in a bowl and pour in half the unsweetened coconut milk. Mix and allow to soak for a few minutes. Process the bread mixture in the food processor for 40 seconds, until it turns into a paste (you may have to keep stopping the processor to push the mixture onto the blades). Remove and set aside.
Place tomato, onion, ginger, coriander, spring onions and Jalapeño in the food processor. Process for 40 seconds or until incorporated. Remove and set aside.
Bring the remaining coconut milk, tomato, onion and spices mixture and dried shrimp to a light boil in a large sauce pan over medium-high heat. Turn the heat down to medium then add the groundnut oil and bread mixture, stirring constantly until the sauce thickens. Cook for 30 minutes over medium-low heat, stirring constantly.
Heat the canola oil in a large frying pan. Once the oil is smoking, add the raw shrimp and sauté for 1½ minutes, until they turn pink and start to curl. Season with salt and pepper.
Transfer the stew to a large serving bowl and cover with fried shrimp. Garnish with chopped coriander and serve immediately with rice.

# 49 - Shrimp Stew (Vatapá) - Brazil

*Note. Original recipes for this dish call for the use of red palm oil. Deforestation to facilitate the production of palm oil is growing at an alarming rate, threatening the habitat of many endangered species. In the interests of conservation, groundnut oil and turmeric have been substituted for palm oil in this recipe.

# 50 - Fried Stuffed Potatoes (Papas Rellenas) - Peru

Peru has a history of civilisation which is one of the oldest in the world, going back some 5,000 years. It is only to be expected that Peruvian cuisine has an equally long and varied history. Indigenous people such as the Incas, had their own methods and ingredients long before the arrival of the Europeans in the 16$^{th}$ century; potatoes and sweet potatoes are native to the Andes and along with corn, chilli peppers and quinoa they formed the basis for many recipes. With the arrival of the Europeans, other ingredients such as rice, wheat, beef and chicken were added to the Peruvian repertoire. Asian methods and ingredients have also had an influence.

This recipe is for a snack which is so filling it can be used as a main meal.

**What you need**

4 large potatoes, peeled and cubed
½ tsp salt
1 tbs vegetable oil
1 onion, chopped
1 green pepper, chopped
3 cloves garlic, minced
450 g minced beef
1 tsp salt
2 tsp ground cumin
1 tsp ground black pepper
4 tsp tomato paste
1 tsp distilled white vinegar
4 eggs
200 g dry bread crumbs
135 g all-purpose flour
vegetable oil for frying

**What to do**

Bring the potatoes to a boil in salted water over a high heat, reduce to medium-low, cover the pan, and simmer until tender (about 20 minutes). Drain and allow to dry for 2 minutes. Mash the potatoes with ½ tsp salt. Allow to cool to room temperature.

Heat 1 tbs of vegetable oil in a large frying pan over medium heat. Add the onion, green pepper, and garlic and cook until the onion has softened and turned translucent. Increase the heat to medium-high and add the minced beef, combining well. Cook until the beef is crumbly and just cooked. Add the salt, cumin, pepper, tomato paste, and vinegar. Stir until the tomato paste has dissolved. Turn out into a bowl and allow to cool to room temperature.

Line a baking sheet with greaseproof paper and set aside.

Beat the eggs in a bowl and set aside.

Pour the bread crumbs and flour into separate, shallow dishes, and set aside.

Once the beef and potatoes have cooled, form the potato balls. Take a handful of the potato, divide into two equal portions. Form each into a small bowl shape and fill with the beef mixture. Place the two halves together, seal the edges, and smooth to make a ball. Roll the ball in the flour to coat, shake off the excess then dip into the beaten egg. Transfer to the breadcrumbs, rolling until completely coated. Gently toss between your hands to allow any loose bread crumbs to fall away. Place the breaded potato balls onto the prepared baking sheet. Refrigerate 2-4 hours or freeze for later use.

Heat the oil in a deep fat fryer or large pan to 175°C.

Cook the potato balls in batches until crispy and golden brown, about 3 minutes. Roll the balls around as they cook to ensure even browning. Drain on a paper towel lined plate before serving.

# 50 - Fried Stuffed Potatoes (Papas Rellenas) - Peru

# 51 - Fish with seafood sauce (Pescado a la parrilla con salsa de marisco) - Ecuador

Ecuador is a multicultural society. Many Central American and Pacific races were already established in the country prior to being absorbed into the Inca culture in the 15$^{th}$ century. In the 16$^{th}$ century, the Spanish arrived and colonised the region. The country gained its independence in the 1800s, but Spanish has remained the official language to this day.

The majority of the 15.2 million population are mestizos, mixed race, being of European and Amerindian descent.

That is reflected in the cuisine, which has both traditional and European influences. Ranging from sea level on the Pacific coast, to high up in the Andes, the country sees many different ingredients utilised. At the higher altitudes beef, chicken and guinea pig feature as well as root crops and grains, whereas in the coastal regions, with their access to sea, fish, shellfish, coconuts and fruits are more common.

This dish is from the coastal region and can be made without the curry if you wish. As usual, adapt the recipe to suit your own tastes.

## What you need

300 g mixture of frozen scallops, shrimp and squid
        OR
1 whole squid, cleaned and cut into rings, 6-8 scallops, 120 g fresh shrimp.

½ medium onion, minced
2 cloves garlic, minced
4 sprigs parsley, leaves plucked, and stems minced (reserve leaves)
3 tbs olive oil
80 ml white grape juice
2 fish fillets, such as halibut, sole or cod (I used sea bream)
salt and freshly ground black pepper to taste
1 tsp curry powder (mild or hot to suit your taste)
80 ml whipping cream

## What to do

If using, thaw the frozen seafood in a refrigerator overnight.

Heat 1 tbs olive oil in large pan. Sauté the onion, garlic, and minced parsley stems, until the onion is becoming translucent.

Add the seafood and sauté for 2-4 minutes, until the shrimp begins to turn pink at edges. Pour in the grape juice. Allow to simmer for 5 minutes over a low heat.

Heat the remaining 2 tbs of olive oil in a frying pan. Cook the fish for 4 minutes on each side. Season with salt and pepper. (Alternatively, barbeque the fish to add a little smokiness to the flavour).

Add the curry powder to the cream, mix well then add to the seafood mixture in the pan. Season seafood curry sauce to taste with salt and pepper and stir in the parsley leaves.

Serve either with the fish in the bottom of shallow dish with the seafood curry sauce poured over the top, or the seafood sauce in the bowl first with the fish on top. Accompany with plain boiled rice.

# 51 - Fish with seafood sauce (Pescado a la parrilla con salsa de marisco) - Ecuador

# 52 - Cheese sticks with avocado dip
# (Tequeños con Guasacaca) - Venezuela

It should come as no surprise, that like many of the other countries in South America, Venezuelan cuisine has been influenced by a number of other nations. Native American and Spanish influences dominate, but other European countries, as well as West Africa, have played their part in the cuisine of this, one of the most northerly countries of the South American continent.

Tequeños are popular throughout Latin America but originated in Venezuela; exactly where is open to discussion.

Please take care when wrapping the cheese with the dough and ensure there is sufficient overlap, otherwise the stick will open up and fall apart when you try to remove it from the oil. That is the voice of experience!

## What you need

### For the sticks

250 g all-purpose flour
½ tsp salt
70 g butter, chilled
1 egg
110 ml water
350 g queso blanco or queso fresco cheese (pg. 110), farmers cheese, or other firm, salty cheese that melts partially (I used Feta for this recipe).
Vegetable oil for frying

### For the dip

2 ripe avocados
Salt and freshly ground pepper to taste
3 tbs vinegar
1 green pepper, diced
1 small onion, finely chopped
3 cloves garlic, finely chopped
1 small mild/sweet chilli pepper (optional), finely chopped
110 ml vegetable or olive oil
40 g chopped tomato (optional)
4 tbs chopped fresh parsley or coriander

## What to do

### For the sticks

Mix the flour and the salt together in a mixing bowl
Chop the butter into 1 cm cubes and add them to the bowl along with the egg.
Use your fingers to mix the egg and butter into the flour until the mixture is sandy and crumbly, and the butter is in very small pieces.
Add the water to the mixture stirring in with a fork. Add more water, 1 tbs at a time, until the mixture starts to come together as a dough. Knead the dough in the bowl, adding more water if overly crumbly. The dough should be soft and malleable but not perfectly blended. Cover with cling film and let rest for 20-30 minutes.
Cut the cheese into sticks about 9 cm long and about 1 cm square.
Roll out half the dough on a lightly floured surface into a 35 cm square. Use a sharp knife or pizza cutter to cut the dough into 2.5 cm wide strips.
Wrap the dough around one of the cheese sticks: Start at one end of the stick and cover the end with dough. Continue to wrap dough around the stick in a spiral fashion, overlapping the edges well, until you reach the other end. Cover the other end of the stick with dough and seal; cut off any excess. (Use a bit of water to help seal the dough). The cheese must not show through anywhere. Repeat with remaining cheese sticks.
Heat the oil in a frying pan and cook the sticks in batches, turning frequently with a spatula, until golden brown. Alternatively, deep fry.
Cover in foil and keep warm in a low temperature oven (150°C), until ready to serve.

# 52 - Cheese sticks with avocado dip
# (Tequeños con Guasacaca) - Venezuela

**For the dip - Guasacaca**

Peel, pit and dice the avocado. Toss with a pinch of salt and the vinegar, in a bowl. Mash until creamy. Add the green pepper and onion and mix well.
Add the garlic and chilli and mix well.
Add the vegetable oil, chopped tomato and the coriander or parsley and combine.
To make a smoother guasacaca, add the oil and vinegar to a blender, then the remaining ingredients in batches and process until smooth.
Season with salt and freshly ground pepper to taste.

# 53 - Shredded beef salad (Salpicón de res) - Panama

Mention Panama and most people will know about the canal and hats. Surprisingly, the hats originated in Ecuador, but the canal is certainly Panamanian. It first opened in August 1914 and is a major source of income for Panama, as well as a boon to shipping companies whose vessels can pass from one side of the Americas to the other, without travelling around Cape Horn.

As we travel north from the South American continent, Panama is the first country we reach in Central America; bordered on one side by the Caribbean, and the other by the Pacific, to the south, Columbia and to the north, Costa Rica.

Originally populated by indigenous tribes, Panama became a Spanish settlement in the 16$^{th}$ century, breaking away from Spanish rule in the early part of the 19$^{th}$ century. By this time, the Spanish influence had been firmly embedded in the cuisine, but as we have seen with other countries throughout the world, this influence was combined with local methods and ingredients. Some of you may not be familiar with the cut of beef in the recipe, but this is one of the tastiest parts, albeit not as tender as some of the other cuts. By cooking for a longer time, we are breaking down the structure of the meat to tenderise it, but still retaining all that flavour.

**What you need**

750 g beef (skirt or flank)
1½ medium onions
3 medium tomatoes
1 romaine lettuce
8 tbs olive oil
2 tbs vinegar
2 tbs lemon juice
1 tsp dried oregano
1 tsp salt
1 avocado, sliced

**What to do**

Place the beef in a pot with about 2 litres of water and the half onion. Bring to the boil then cover and simmer until tender, about 1½ hours.
Remove the meat from the water and allow to cool to room temperature. Break the meat with your fingers to form strands, removing any fat or skin. Reserve the broth for another use (can be stored in the freezer).
Cut the whole onion into thin slices, chop the tomatoes and cut the lettuce in thin strips.
Mix the olive oil, vinegar, lemon juice, oregano and salt with a hand beater or use an electric blender to form a dressing.
Mix the shredded beef and sliced onion in a bowl and add half the dressing, combine well. Add the chopped tomatoes, lettuce and remaining dressing. Stir everything thoroughly, using 2 large spoons.
Slice the avocado and place the slices in the salad.
Serve immediately. Accompany with toast or crackers and some pickled chillies or carrots. I served with corn on the cob.

**Variations.**

Use chicken instead of beef.
Add any vegetables to hand: sliced radish, grated raw carrot or cooked in cubes, cooked corn kernels, boiled peas, etc.
Use guacamole instead of the dressing and leave out the avocado.

# 53 - Shredded beef salad (Salpicón de res) - Panama

Serve your salpicón as 'tacos': leave the lettuce leaves whole. Combine all other ingredients. then place some of the mixture on each leaf and eat the 'tacos' with your hands.

# 54 - Casado - Costa Rica

The history of the land is often the first thing mentioned in these recipes, illustrating how each region has been influenced by cuisine from other countries. Costa Rica is no exception in this respect, and like much of Central and Southern America, they found themselves coming under Spanish rule in the 16th century.

But it is the vision for the future that is the remarkable aspect of Costa Rica. The country intends to be carbon-neutral by 2021, has banned recreational hunting and is one of the leading nations when it comes to protecting the environment (around 25% of the country is protected by national park or protected area status). Costa Rica has around 5% of the world's biodiversity making it an important area for wildlife conservation.

With lush, tropical rainforests, golden beaches and dramatic volcanic vistas, the Costa Ricans are right to proudly boast a Pura Vida - pure life.

## What you need

4 chicken breasts
salt and pepper, to taste
2 garlic cloves, crushed
vegetable oil, for frying
120 ml beef broth
2 ripe plantains, peeled and sliced
1 small head of lettuce (Iceberg)
1 tomato, sliced
1 carrot, grated
vinaigrette dressing (see recipe from Panama)
450 g rice, cooked (180 g uncooked weight)
400 g black beans (turtle beans), cooked (200 g if using dried beans)
4 eggs, fried or hard boiled
120 g queso fresco, sliced (see recipe below)
tortillas

## What to do

If using dried beans, be prepared to let them cook for 1-3 hours first (they don't need an overnight soak if you do this).

Prepare the salad by combining the grated carrot and tomato slices. Season with salt, pepper and vinaigrette; set aside.

Season the chicken with the salt, pepper and garlic. Heat 2 tbs of vegetable oil in a frying pan over a medium heat and cook the chicken on each side. Deglaze the pan with the beef broth and bring to a boil. Reduce by a third then set aside.

In a separate frying pan, fry the plantain slices in a little oil until golden-brown.

Reheat the beans in the reserved broth.

Warm tortillas in the oven then fold into a cone, fill with some of the beans and put on a plate.

Add the prepared portions side-by-side: one piece of chicken, fried plantains to the side, followed by salad, rice, one fried or hard-boiled egg and some slices of queso fresco.

## To make Queso Fresco

### What you need

2 litres whole milk
3-4 tbs white vinegar
sea salt

# 54 - Casado - Costa Rica

**What to do**

Heat the milk in a medium saucepan and bring to the boil. Add 1 tbs of salt. Turn the heat to low then add 3 tbs of distilled white vinegar, 1 tbs at a time, while stirring. The milk will separate into curds and whey. If not, add one more tbs of vinegar. Continue to stir gently to encourage the curd formation.

Drain into a cheesecloth-lined colander or sieve, over a pan. Let sit for 5-10 minutes, until the cheese is cool enough to handle. Form the curds into a ball or disc while squeezing excess whey through the cheesecloth. The cheese is ready to eat now, but to make a drier, firmer cheese, set it on a plate or baking tin with a plate on top of it. Use a weight - cans, pans, books or jars - to press it down for between 15 minutes to 2 hours.

Herbs and spices can be added before pressing, mixing well with the curds.

# 55 - Berenjenas Rellenas - Nicaragua

Nicaragua is the largest country in Central America. In keeping with the other countries of this region, there is a strong Spanish influence on the cuisine, which centres around local fruits and vegetables as well as seafood and coconuts; the latter being more prominent on the Caribbean coast.

A common dish in Nicaragua and throughout the region, is Gallo Pinto. This combination of rice and red or black beans, is often eaten for breakfast, lunch and dinner and can have ingredients added to it for variation.

This recipe uses a vegetable that will be familiar to you, the aubergine or eggplant. Feel free to substitute the meat with other vegetables if you prefer.

## What you need

2 aubergines (about 250 g each)
200 g minced chicken or beef
100 g beef bacon in strips
2 medium tomatoes, finely chopped and crushed
¼ onion
½ green pepper
30 g grated cheese such as cheddar
olive oil
salt and black pepper

### For the béchamel sauce

25 g butter
25 g all-purpose flour
250 ml milk

## What to do

Preheat the oven to 180°C. Cut the aubergines in half lengthways and with a knife make deep cuts in the flesh, ensuring not to break through the skin. Put the 4 halves on an oven tray, skin side down. Brush each half with a little oil and add a pinch of salt. Bake in the oven for 30 minutes.

Finely chop the onion and green pepper. Heat 4 tbs oil in a frying pan and sauté the onion for 2 minutes, adding a pinch of salt to season. Add the pepper to the pan and cook for a further 4 minutes

When the pepper is ready add the minced meat to the frying pan, breaking up into individual grains as it cooks. Season again with a pinch of salt and cook for 5 minutes until just cooked through.

In a separate pan, brown the bacon until crisp. When done, break into smaller pieces then add to the onion, peppers and minced meat.

When the aubergines are ready, remove from the oven and allow to cool enough to be handled. Using a spoon, remove the flesh from the aubergine, taking care not to break the skin. Break the flesh into small pieces then add to the pan with the meat and onion mixture. Cook for 5 minutes. Add the tomato and cook for a further 8 minutes. Remove from the heat, add salt and black pepper to taste. Set aside.

Melt the butter in a pan then stir in the flour to form a smooth roux. Cook for a little less than 1 minute. Add the milk a little at a time, stirring constantly. Bring to the boil. The mixture should thicken and become glossy. Continue to boil for 2 minutes.

Stuff the aubergines with the meat mixture then distribute the béchamel over the aubergine halves. Sprinkle with the grated cheese.

Bake for 10 minutes at 185°C. During the final 4 minutes, switch on the oven grill (if your oven supports it), to further melt the cheese and crisp slightly.

## 55 - Berenjenas Rellenas - Nicaragua

# 56 - Beef in Tomato and Pepper Sauce (Carne en Jocón) - Guatemala

There is evidence of civilisation in Guatemala dating back many thousands of years; the earliest settlers being hunter-gatherers. Pollen found in the soil from approximately 5,500 years ago, indicates the population were growing corn, suggesting farming methods had been introduced even then.

Some 4,500 years ago, the Maya started to form small settlements and grow crops, establishing themselves around water sources.

Around 2,700 years ago, the Mayan culture was firmly in place; cities were established and widespread cultivation of the staple foods of the Mayan diet, chilli peppers, beans, maize and squashes was evident.

There is no universally accepted theory as to why, but in the $9^{th}$ century, the Mayan culture collapsed, and the cities were abandoned, but the Mayan people remained present.

As we have seen in other countries, the Spanish settled the region in the $16^{th}$ century, bringing their own methods and ingredients which have been incorporated into the cuisine and stripping away much of the Mayan culture. However, there is still a Mayan presence to this day, especially in the Guatemalan Highlands where the Spanish influence did not extend.

This dish incorporates some of the Mayan staples and beef, which was almost certainly introduced by the Spanish.

## What you need

3 tbs oil (olive or groundnut)
1 onion chopped
2 cloves garlic, finely chopped
1 red or green bell pepper seeded & chopped
2 Serrano peppers, chopped (can be replaced by your choice of chilli peppers, Jalapeño, Habanero, etc).
1.3 kg lean boneless beef cut into cubes
10 Mexican green tomatoes (tomatillos) **(see Cook's tip)**
3 med tomatoes peeled and coarsely chopped
1 bay leaf
½ tsp salt
½ tsp pepper
¼ tsp ground cloves
1 tsp oregano
175 ml beef stock
2 medium tortillas

## What to do

Heat the oil in heavy saucepan and sauté the onion, garlic and peppers until the onion is soft. Add the meat and cook until browned. Add the remaining ingredients except the tortillas.

The liquid should barely cover the meat. Add a little more stock if necessary. Cover and simmer gently until the beef is tender, about 2 hours.

Soak the tortillas in cold water, and crumble like bread crumbs. Add to the pan and simmer uncovered, until the sauce is thickened.

Serve on plain rice.

## Cook's tip:

Tomatillos can be hard to locate. They are like green tomatoes, but smaller and have a distinctive tart taste to them. To substitute, use 2 medium green tomatoes with 1 tbs salsa verde or 1 tbs lime juice. It won't be quite the same but as close as we are going to get without the original ingredient.

# 56 - Beef in Tomato and Pepper Sauce (Carne en Jocón) - Guatemala

# 57 - Curried Goat - Jamaica

Jamaica has a rich and varied history. This Caribbean island nation is thought to have been settled in the 7th century by nearby islanders. In the 9th century, the Taíno people arrived, probably from South America, via the eastern islands. The Spanish visited in the 15th century but it was considered to be of little value, other than as a military base, which they established.

Recognising its strategic importance, the British attacked the island, gaining control from the Spanish in the 17th century. At the invitation of the governor, pirates, or privateers as they were known, were invited to make the island their base. In return, they would attack Spanish owned vessels, defending the island in return for a share of the spoils.

In the same period, sugarcane was introduced to the Caribbean by the Dutch, and farmers were encouraged to switch to growing sugar, rather than tobacco and cotton. This paved the way for a flourishing sugar industry, so that by the early part of the 18th century it had replaced piracy as the main source of income. The labour-intensive nature of sugarcane cultivation caused the British to bring hundreds of thousands of slaves from Africa to work in the plantations.

The resultant mixture of races and cultures, combined with the abundance of crops introduced from South East Asia, brought by other settlers, has resulted in a fusion of cuisine like no other. This recipe is easy to make, but takes several hours, and you should consider cooking over 2 days.

## What you need

1 kg goat meat (buy shoulder with bone in. Get the butcher to de-bone but keep the bones).
juice ½ lime
2 tbs mild curry powder
2 tbs all-purpose seasoning
6 tbs oil (sunflower or groundnut)
425 ml stock **(see Cook's tip)**
1 onion, roughly chopped
2 cm root ginger, finely chopped
1 hot red chilli (Scotch Bonnet or Habanero), seeds in and chopped
2 garlic cloves, finely chopped
10 allspice berries
½ red pepper, deseeded and cubed
½ green pepper, deseeded and cubed
2 spring onions, green part only, roughly chopped
2 tbs flat-leaf parsley, chopped
2 tbs fresh coriander, chopped
2 potatoes cut into large chunks
salt and pepper to taste

## What to do

Wash and pat dry the meat. Cut into large chunks. Mix the lime juice, curry powder and all-purpose seasoning in a large bowl. Add the meat and ensure well coated with the mix. Cover, and leave to marinate in a fridge for 4 hours.

Heat a large heavy saucepan over a high heat then add the oil. When hot, add the meat mixture. Mix the meat and oil using a wooden spoon to ensure the meat is well coated. Cover the pan and lower the heat and simmer for 45 minutes, checking occasionally to ensure the meat is not sticking to the pan.

Add 150 ml of stock to the pan and simmer for 45 minutes, then add another 150 ml stock and cook for a further 45 minutes.

Add the ginger, onion, chilli, garlic and all spice, stir until combined then add all the other ingredients except the potatoes. Bring to the boil then simmer covered for 1 hour 40 minutes.

# 57 - Curried Goat - Jamaica

Check frequently and add more stock if necessary. Finally, add the potato and cook for a further 20 minutes.
Serve with either boiled rice or Jamaican rice and peas.

**Cook's tip:**

To make the stock; cover the bones with water and bring to the boil. Simmer for 20-30 minutes. Drain, discard the water, then cover with fresh water. Bring back to the boil, add one tsp of salt and simmer for 2 hours. Reserve the stock for later use.

# 58 - Crab in Creole Sauce (Cangrejos Enchilados) - Cuba

Cuba and Jamaica are close neighbours in the Caribbean, so it will be no surprise their cuisine is similar. Taíno, Spanish, African and, to a certain degree, Chinese techniques have influenced the type of food and cooking in Cuba.

Since 1962 certain basic ingredients can only be obtained by presenting a coupon which limits the amount of a particular product that can be purchased. Clearly, this will have an effect on the cuisine, yet the food is vibrant and tasty. Cubans generally serve the dishes in one go and not as individual courses.

Typical ingredients are; sugar, rice, wheat, beans, potatoes, bananas, mango, coffee, garlic and onion. From Africa came yam, cocoyam, plantain, okra and the Guinea chicken, also known as Guinea Fowl, all of which had an impact on the local recipes.

This melting pot of cultures and ingredients resulted in a quite distinctive flavour which is notable not only in the Caribbean Islands, but in some of the southern states of the USA, such as Louisiana; you will have no doubt heard of it - Creole. The origin and meaning of this word is much disputed and it doesn't only describe the food, but also the people and culture.

This recipe is a one-pot dish, a bonus if you are a messy cook.

## What you need

3 tbs olive oil
3 large cloves garlic, finely chopped
1 large onion, finely chopped
400 g chopped tomatoes
1 tbs tomato paste
1 bay leaf
100 ml cider vinegar
100 ml water
2 tbs sugar
120 ml finely chopped drained pimiento
1 tbs Worcestershire Sauce
salt and freshly ground black pepper to taste
1 seeded hot chilli pepper, finely chopped, or a pepper sauce to taste
3 tbs finely chopped fresh parsley for garnish (optional)
juice of 1 lime
1 kg crabmeat, picked over to remove any cartilage

## What to do

Heat a large saucepan or frying pan over low heat until the oil is fragrant, add the garlic and onion. Cook until tender, stirring all the while (6-8 minutes). Add the tomatoes, tomato paste, bay leaf, cider vinegar, water, sugar, pimientos, Worcestershire Sauce, salt, pepper, and chilli. Cook until the mixture has thickened. 5 minutes before serving, add the crabmeat and lime juice and cook over low heat until the crabmeat is heated. Transfer to a plate or serving bowl, garnish with parsley, and serve immediately, accompanied by steamed rice.

# 58 - Crab in Creole Sauce (Cangrejos Enchilados) - Cuba

# 59 - Huevos Rancheros - Mexico

Mention Mexican cuisine and most will think of intense flavours and spices: with good reason. The chilli pepper is thought to have originated in what we now know as Mexico, some 6,000 years ago. Prior to the arrival of Columbus in the 15th century, Aztec and Mayan cuisine was well developed. When the Conquistadores came to Mexico and brought their own produce, the traditional recipes blended well with the new ingredients; many of the recipes in existence today in Mexico, date from the pre-Columbian period.

This recipe probably dates from later as farming became more organised. Even the non-Spanish speakers amongst us can probably hazard a guess that the dish has a connection with ranching and they wouldn't be wrong. The literal translation is 'ranchers' eggs'. Originally served as a mid-morning meal on the large rural farms in Mexico, the dish is no longer the preserve of ranchers, gaining popularity throughout Mexico and further afield.

As one would imagine with a recipe of this sort, there are a number of variations; Huevos divorciados (divorced eggs), uses different salsas for each egg. Then there is the addition of cheese; something that isn't in the original recipe, but I have to confess liking it so much, I couldn't leave it out. Traditionally, the dish would be served with refried beans and Mexican rice.

**What you need**

2 tbs olive oil
1 medium onion, finely chopped
2 cloves garlic finely chopped
3 medium tomatoes, finely chopped
1 medium Jalapeño chilli, finely chopped
½ tsp hot sauce
salt and freshly ground pepper
4 tbs olive oil
4 x 6-inch corn tortillas
4 large eggs
125 g queso fresco

**What to do**

### Method 1

Heat the oil in a frying pan and cook the onion and garlic until soft. Add the tomatoes, Jalapeño, sauce, salt and pepper and continue to cook over a medium low heat for a few minutes to create a salsa.

In the meantime, heat the 4 tbs of olive oil in another frying pan and fry the tortillas until crispy. Place the tortillas in a warm oven.

Fry the eggs in the same oil until just done. Put the salsa mixture on the tortillas, then top with the eggs. Sprinkle with queso fresco and serve immediately.

### Method 2

Prepare the salsa as above. Place the fried tortillas in a shallow casserole and top with the salsa mixture, Break an egg onto each tortilla on top of the salsa. Sprinkle with the queso fresco. Place the casserole in a preheated oven at 180°C and bake for 15 minutes. Serve immediately.

# 59 - Huevos Rancheros - Mexico

# 60 - Fajitas - USA

Fajitas is a dish with a recent history and one which is reasonably documented. On many occasions, in this book, we see how an influx of people from another culture influences the cuisine of a country, and here we have a prime example.

Fajitas are the result of Mexican ranch workers crossing the Rio Grande into Texas to seek employment on the ranches. In the late 1930s to the early 1940s, the Mexican workers were often paid in part with the least desirable cuts of meat, in this case, skirt, which is tougher than some of the other cuts, but is full of flavour. The ranch hands marinated and grilled the steak, which they knew as arracheras.

In the late 1960s, the food had gained popularity outside of the ranches, but it wasn't until the 1970s that the term 'fajitas' was adopted. This came from the Spanish word faja, which means belt or girdle. Who first coined the term is open to dispute, but by the late 1970s it was firmly established, as was the dish in the USA.

Nowadays, the term has come to mean anything that is cooked and rolled up in a soft flour tortilla, but a true fajita is made from beef skirt.

In this recipe, I used flank which is the cut adjacent to the skirt and is equally as tasty.

## What you need

750 g steak (skirt or flank)
2 tbs olive oil
1 tbs lime juice
1 garlic clove, finely minced
½ tsp chilli powder
½ tsp cumin
½ tsp hot pepper flakes
½ tsp black pepper
½ tsp salt
8 flour tortillas (20 cm)
1-2 onions, (enough to make a good mix with the peppers)
2 small sweet peppers, (green, red, or yellow)

## What to do

Slice the steak into thin strips.

Mix together 1 tbs olive oil, lime juice, garlic, chilli powder, cumin, hot pepper flakes, black pepper and salt in a bowl. Add the beef and stir to coat, cover and set aside in a fridge for about an hour.

Wrap the tortillas in foil and place in 175°C oven for 5-10 minutes or until heated through.

Cut the onions in half lengthways then slice into strips. Cut the peppers into strips.

Heat the remaining olive oil in large non-stick frying pan, over medium high heat.

Add the onions and peppers. Stir-fry for 3-4 minutes, until softened; transfer to a bowl and set aside.

Add the beef strips to the pan and stir-fry for 3-4 minutes or until they lose their red colour.

Return the onions and peppers to the pan; continue to stir-fry for 2 minutes.

Serve with guacamole, salsa and sour cream. Rice, and refried beans can be served on the side.

To prepare the Fajita, spoon a portion of the beef mixture down the centre of each tortilla, top with your desired toppings, fold bottom of tortilla up over filling, fold the sides in, overlapping, to produce a wrapped parcel of food.

Be prepared to have juices on your chin and hands!

# 60 - Fajitas - USA

# 61 - Prawn Gumbo - USA

Gumbo, a dish from the southern United States, is often cited as an example of the melting-pot nature of the cultures of Louisiana.

The word gumbo possibly derives from a Bantu word for okra, ki ngombo, or ngumbo, suggesting the dish has some connection with the Africans brought to the USA as slaves. On the other hand, one ingredient which is often used, ground sassafras leaves (also known as gumbo filé), is known as kombo by the Choctaw Native Americans, suggesting the dish may have other origins. The roux which is used as a thickening agent for the dish in some recipes, is undoubtedly French, although much darker than a normal roux, pointing to a Cajun input.

As with some other dishes we have encountered on our journey, there are many different recipes for gumbo, some using the roux for thickening, some using okra instead (this one uses both). Some versions are made with chicken, some seafood, while others use sausage and when it comes to using tomatoes there are two camps, just as there are for creole sauces.

One common aspect in all the recipes is the use of what the Louisiana people call the 'Holy trinity' of vegetables, onion, celery and bell peppers.

Whatever method is used, there can be no doubt this is a tasty and filling dish.

**What you need**

65 g all-purpose flour
85 g butter
2 sticks celery, finely chopped
1 medium onion, finely chopped
1 medium green pepper, finely chopped
2 cloves garlic, minced
250 g smoked beef sausage, sliced
1.4 litres water
3 cubes beef stock
2 tsp white sugar
1 tbs hot pepper sauce, or to taste
½ tsp Cajun seasoning, or to taste
2 bay leaves
½ tsp dried thyme leaves
400 g stewed tomatoes
135 g tomato puree
1 tbs melted butter
280 g okra, sliced
1 tbs distilled white vinegar
1 kg uncooked medium shrimp, peeled and deveined
1 tbs Worcestershire sauce

**What to do**

Make a roux by whisking the flour and the butter together in a large, heavy saucepan over medium to medium-low heat to form a smooth mixture. Cook the roux, stirring constantly, until it turns a rich mahogany brown colour. This can take 20-30 minutes or longer; watch carefully and stir constantly or it will burn. Remove from the heat; continue stirring until the mixture stops cooking. Stir the celery, onion, green pepper and garlic into the roux. Mix in the sausage. Add some of the water to allow the mixture to a simmer over medium-low heat. Cook until vegetables are tender. Remove from heat and set aside.

Bring the remaining water to the boil in a large pan or soup pot and add the beef stock cubes. Stir until the cubes dissolve then stir the roux mixture into the boiling water, reduce the heat to a

# 61 - Prawn Gumbo - USA

simmer. Add the sugar, salt, hot pepper sauce, Cajun seasoning, bay leaves, thyme, stewed tomatoes, and tomato puree. Simmer over low heat for 1 hour.

Meanwhile, melt 1 tbs of butter in a frying pan and cook the okra with the vinegar over medium heat for 15 minutes; remove with slotted spoon then stir into the simmering gumbo with the Worcestershire sauce, and simmer for a further 45 minutes to an hour. Mix in the shrimp and cook for 5 more minutes.

Serve on a bed of steamed rice.

**Cook's tip:**

The longer the gumbo is left to simmer, the more intense the flavours will become, but stir frequently to avoid it 'sticking' to the bottom of the pan.

# 62 - Apache Fried Rabbit with Corn, Blueberry & Wild Rice Salad - USA

Throughout our journey, it has been difficult to establish original recipes of a region owing to the influence of immigrants bringing other ingredients and methods.

The Native American tribes of North America can trace their roots back to well before Columbus arrived on their shores and may have been on the continent for 3,0000 years.

Traditionally hunter-gatherers, they lived off what the land could provide, gathering the native crops; maize, squash, beans and turnips and hunting wildlife; deer, rabbits, ducks, turkeys and buffalo.

They understood the land and their own part in the natural world; never over hunting or cropping, moving from place to place to allow the land to recover. They could be considered to be early conservationists. The lifestyle was simple yet effective.

Both the dishes in this recipe are as authentic as we can establish in this day and age and have probably remained the same over hundreds of years.

## What you need

1 prepared rabbit
4 tbs duck or goose fat
50 g all-purpose flour
½ tsp salt
water sufficient to cover rabbit pieces

## For the salad

180 g wild rice
430 ml water
¼ tsp salt
2 litres water
1 tsp salt
6 ears sweet corn, husked (or 250 frozen corn)
1 Jalapeño pepper, seeded and finely chopped (leave the seeds in if you like it a little bit hotter)
100 g fresh blueberries
4 tbs lime juice
4 tbs olive oil
1 small cucumber, finely diced
2 tbs honey or maple syrup
1 small red onion, chopped
½ tsp ground cumin
1 small bunch fresh coriander, chopped

## What to do

### To prepare the rabbit

Wash the rabbit then cut into portions and cover with water. Bring to a boil then simmer for 2 hours.

Sieve together the salt and flour onto a deep plate.

Remove the rabbit from the water and dip into the flour mixture, coating evenly. Heat the fat in a frying pan and cook the rabbit pieces until golden brown.

### To prepare the salad

Add the rice, ¼ tsp salt and 230 ml water to a pan. Bring to the boil then simmer for 25-30 minutes (wild rice takes longer to cook than Asian rice). Don't worry if not all the water is absorbed. Check

# 62 - Apache Fried Rabbit with Corn, Blueberry & Wild Rice Salad - USA

the rice has split open and is tender. You can reduce the cooking time if you like the rice to be a little bit crunchy. Remove with a slotted spoon and allow to cool.

Bring the 2 litres of water to a boil in a large pan. Add the ears of corn and salt (refer to the packet if using frozen corn). Cook covered for 5 minutes, or until tender. When cool enough to handle, cut the kernels from the cobs. Allow to cool.

In a serving bowl, combine the corn, Jalapeño, blueberries, lime juice, oil, cucumber, honey or maple syrup, red onion, cumin, coriander, and wild rice.

Serve on a plate, topped with the rabbit.

**Cook's tip:**

Wild rice is a species of grass and is not directly related to Asian rice, although it is a cousin. Wild rice has a chewy outer sheath and a slightly nutty flavour.

# 63 - Mom's Apple Pie - USA

'As American as apple pie', is a saying you will often hear to suggest something is as American as it could possibly be. The phrase can trace its roots back to the mid 1800s, although American apple pie is much older. Decades later, when soldiers were asked why they were fighting World War II, a common reply was 'for mom and apple pie.'

Despite this seemingly overwhelming evidence that apple pie is American, the origin of apple pie is almost certainly European, with the earliest known recipe coming from Britain in 1381. Despite this, Americans have taken to this tasty dish wholeheartedly.

The pie as we know it now, would not be the same as the early settlers would know, in what became the United States. The pastry then was made from coarse flour and suet, and the crust would be thick, tough, and virtually inedible. When butter was introduced to the recipe, probably by the French, then the pastry became lighter and more delicate than its predecessor.

Whatever the origin, apple pie with custard, cream, ice cream or even on its own, is a firm favourite, either as a dessert or just to add a bit of luxury to the day.

## What you need

320 g flour
225 g unsalted butter, cold and cubed
1 tsp salt
1 tsp sugar
60-120 ml ice water
1 tbs ground cinnamon
1 tsp ground nutmeg
250 g sugar
2 tbs flour
8 apples, peeled & sliced, half Granny Smith, half Macintosh, or similar **(see Cook's tip)**
30 g butter, cold and sliced
1 egg, lightly beaten
1 tbs sugar
½ tsp cinnamon

## What to do

In a food processor combine the 320 g flour, salt, 1 tsp sugar and use the pulse setting. Add in the 225 g of butter and slowly add the ice water. Pulse until dough just comes together.

If working the pastry by hand knead lightly until all ingredients are combined and no more. Don't overwork the dough or it will make a tough pastry.

Cut the dough into two equal sections. Form into discs and wrap in food wrap. Refrigerate for 1 hour.

Preheat the oven to 200°C.

In a small mixing bowl, combine the cinnamon, nutmeg, 250 g sugar and 2 tbs flour, set aside. In a large mixing bowl, add the peeled and sliced apples. Sprinkle the spice and flour mixture over the apples and toss to coat.

Roll out one disc of dough on a lightly floured surface, large enough to cover your pie tin. Shape to fit, cutting off any excess.

Place the apple mixture into the pie pan, making the centre slightly raised and then add 2 tbs of sliced butter to the top of the mixture. Roll out the second disc large enough to fit the top of the pie leaving an overhang. Place the pie dough on top of apple mixture and crimp edges to seal. Cut four slits in the crust and lightly brush egg wash on top. Mix together 1 tbs of sugar with the ½ tsp of cinnamon then sprinkle liberally on the crust.

# 63 - Mom's Apple Pie - USA

Place onto a baking tray and cook for approximately 50 minutes or until golden brown and bubbly. Allow to pie to rest until cool before slicing.

**Cook's tip:**

Fill a bowl with enough water to cover the apple slices. Slice a lemon or lime and add to the water. The citric acid in the water will stop your apple slices from going brown, whilst you prepare the rest of the ingredients.

# 64 - Venison and Sweet Potato Dauphinoise - Canada

In keeping with its neighbour to the south, Canadian cuisine has been greatly influenced by the nations who first populated the country, mainly England, Scotland and France. Prior to this, aboriginal foods would be a mixture of ingredients obtained from foraging, hunting and to a certain degree, farming.

Fish and wild mammals were staples, both of which were eaten fresh, as well as processed in various ways to preserve them.

Venison was often obtained from the white-tailed deer, moose, elk and caribou and is still eaten by many Canadians outside the urban areas.

## What you need

### For the venison

2 tbs of fresh thyme leaves
5 dried juniper berries
sea salt and freshly ground black pepper
4 tbs olive oil
500 g-1 kg venison loin or steaks (**see Cook's tip**)
4 shallots, peeled and finely sliced
1 clove of garlic, peeled and finely sliced
230 ml red grape juice
2 tbs butter

### For the apple chutney

2 tbs olive oil
1 onion, thinly sliced
2 clove garlic, minced
½ tsp chilli flakes
4 tbs red wine vinegar
4 tbs honey
1 tbs Dijon mustard
120 g baking apples, or any tart, green apple
1 tsp thyme, chopped

### For the sweet potato Dauphinoise

butter (to rub inside the dish)
2 sweet potatoes, peeled, thinly sliced into rounds
2 tbs thyme, chopped
2 shallots, sliced
125 g Gruyere or Emmental cheese, grated
350 ml double cream
salt and pepper

### For the honey roasted carrots

170 g baby carrots, peeled
2 tbs olive oil
2 tbs honey
salt and freshly ground black pepper, to taste

### For the rosemary roasted beets

6 medium red beets
4 clove garlic, minced
3 tbs rosemary, chopped
2 tbs olive oil
salt and pepper
1 tbs parsley, chopped

## What to do

### For the venison

Use either a spice mill or mortar and pestle to finely chop or crush the thyme and juniper berries, along with a pinch of salt and pepper. Transfer to a baking dish. Add the olive oil and mix together. Pat the venison dry with some kitchen paper then cover with the oil mixture. Refrigerate for 1-2 hours.

Heat a large frying pan over medium-high heat, sear the venison on all sides for about 8-10 minutes for medium cooked meat, (ideally use a meat thermometer for an internal temperature of 140-150°C. Anything higher and the meat will start to become dry. This will give a medium-rare meat). Remove from the pan, cover with foil and allow to rest for a few minutes. Reduce the heat to medium, add 2 tbs of olive oil, shallots and garlic. Cook until translucent. Increase the heat, add the grape juice, simmer until reduced by half, then remove from the heat. Add the butter and stir until melted. Season to taste.

# 64 - Venison and Sweet Potato Dauphinoise - Canada

### For the apple chutney

Add the oil, onion and garlic to a large sauté pan over medium-high heat. Cook until the onion is golden brown. Add the chilli, vinegar, honey and mustard, apples and thyme. Simmer for 20 minutes. Season with salt and freshly ground black pepper.

### For the sweet potato Dauphinoise

Rub the inside of a casserole dish with the butter. Add the sweet potato slices until the bottom is covered. Season the layer with shallot slices, thyme, salt and pepper. Sprinkle with grated Gruyere. Repeat the layers ending with a layer of seasoned sweet potatoes. Pour the cream over. Cover with foil and bake at 175°C for 40-50 minutes or until the potatoes are tender.

### For the honey roasted baby carrots

Preheat the oven to 220°C. Bring salted water to a boil in a large steamer. Steam the carrots until just tender, about 5 minutes. Drain and place in a bowl. Toss with the oil, honey, salt and pepper. Put the carrots on a baking sheet in a single layer and bake for 10 minutes. Season with salt and freshly ground black pepper.

### For the rosemary roasted beets

Mix 1 tbs of the oil with the garlic, rosemary, salt and pepper. Cut the beet tops almost through to form a hinged lid, then place on a baking tray. Spoon the mixture onto the cut surface of the beets then fold the top back over. Roast at 200°C until tender, about 1 hour.
Carefully peel and trim the hot beets then cut into 5 mm thick slices. Drizzle with remaining oil. Sprinkle with parsley.

### To serve

Slice the venison into 2 cm thick slices before serving. Garnish with the sauce and apple chutney.

### Cook's tip:

Should you be unable to find venison, then you can substitute a very lean beef or buffalo in the recipe.

# 65 - Summer Casserole - Greenland

Greenland is the world's largest island (excluding Australia, which is considered to be a continent), and it is perhaps the world's most inaptly named place too. Over 80% of the island is covered with ice and is second only to Antarctica in terms of the size of the ice sheet. There is much speculation as to how the island came to be named. Some suggest it was an exiled Viking, Erik the Red, who named it Greenland in an effort to get other Vikings to come and settle, while others think he landed on the southern shores in the summer, when the land is green. Some think it is merely an error in translation from the word 'grunt' meaning ground.

The Inuit people are believed to have been the earliest settlers, followed in the late 10th century by the Vikings. It is thought the Vikings cleared away much of the trees and used the land for raising sheep and goats. As would be expected in such a place, the opportunity for growing crops is somewhat limited and restricted to the southern regions. Just when this form of agriculture first took place is unclear. Hunting and fishing would be the primary source of food for both Inuit and Viking alike, although the Vikings had the advantage of regular trade with other settlements.

Many of the recipes from the region owe their origins to the early hunters and fishermen but have been modified over the years as more ingredients became available with the advent of modern agricultural methods, allowing the growing of crops that would previously have been impossible.

## What you need

1 kg halibut, or any firm white fish such as cod
juice from 2 lemons
2 tbs butter
1 large onion, diced
½ small celeriac, peeled and cut into 2.5 cm cubes
1 large leek, washed and sliced
1 carrot, peeled and diced
200 ml white grape juice
1 tbs white wine vinegar
300 ml fish stock
2 egg yolks
150 ml whipping cream (>35% fat content)
salt and fresh grated nutmeg, to taste

## What to do

Dice the fish then place in a dish, cover in lemon juice and set aside.

In a large heavy pan, melt the butter. Add the diced onion, celeriac, leek, and carrots. Stir until all ingredients are coated with the butter. Cover and cook until the vegetables are slightly tender (around 10 minutes). Add the fish, grape juice, vinegar and stock. Cover and bring to a simmer. Cook for another 15 minutes.

In a medium sized bowl, whisk together the egg yolks and the cream, adding a pinch of salt. Take 150 ml of the liquid from the pan and stir it into the cream mixture. Slowly add the mixture to the pan over the fish and vegetables. Cover and cook for a further 5 minutes. Remove the lid, season with salt and nutmeg, to taste.

Serve immediately.

## 65 - Summer Casserole - Greenland

# 66 - Lamb soup (Kjotsupa) - Iceland

Iceland is an island of approximately 103,000 square kilometres, which is 2.5 times larger than Denmark, the country that once ruled this North Atlantic island. Despite this, the population of Iceland is a mere 0.6% of its former ruler and it makes Iceland the most sparsely populated country in Europe.

According to ancient manuscripts, the earliest settlers were Vikings, who came to the island in 874 CE, and it is home to one of the world's earliest functioning legislative assemblies.

Being an island, it is no surprise the sea was a major source of ingredients for Icelandic cuisine, and up to WWII, Iceland relied heavily on subsistence fishing and agriculture. The majority of this agriculture centred on the raising of livestock, with lamb and dairy products being at the fore. Despite having a cold climate and a relatively short growing season, hardier vegetables such as potatoes, kale, turnips and cabbage are often grown and will be found in many of the more traditional recipes. Herbs and spices were rarely used. Other ingredients, which are less familiar to us are shark, whale and walrus. Seabirds also feature, with puffin being considered a delicacy amongst the Icelandic people.

Modern day methods, such as greenhouses and artificial lighting, have introduced more fruit and vegetables into the Icelandic cuisine. Even bananas can be grown this way, although they are not grown on a commercial scale.

The relatively long cooking time for this soup allows the flavours of the ingredients to develop in the stock and produces a heart-warming dish, which I am sure would have welcomed home many an Icelandic fisherman.

## What you need

2.5 litres water
1 kg lamb chops, or 1 kg lamb shoulder, bone in, cut into 4 cm pieces across the bone (ask your butcher to do this for you)
1 onion, thinly sliced
1 large turnip or swede, cut into 2 cm cubes
3 large potatoes cut into 2 cm cubes
3 carrots, cut into 2 cm cubes
2 leeks, sliced
5 thyme sprigs
2 fresh bay leaves
30 g rolled oats
100 g kale, shredded

## What to do

Place the water, lamb and onion in a large saucepan and bring to a simmer over medium-high heat. Skim any impurities from the surface. Season with salt and pepper, then reduce the heat to allow a slow simmer and cook for 1 hour.

Add the vegetables, thyme and bay leaves and cook for a further 1½ hours or until meat is starting to fall off the bone. During this time, add more water if necessary.

Remove the meat and set aside to cool.

Add the oats and cook for 15 minutes or until cooked through.

Shred the meat from the bones and return to soup. Discard the bones.

Stir through kale and season the soup to taste.

## 66 - Lamb soup (Kjotsupa) - Iceland

# 67 - Scrambled eggs and smoked salmon on Kneippbrød- Norway

The origins of smoking food to preserve it probably dates back to the days of the caveman when meat would be hung to dry. Smoke would affect the meat closest to the fires, altering the taste and improving the longevity of the meat.

Just when this process was used on fish is unclear. It is known the Native Americans have used the process for many centuries, as have the Scandinavians, particularly in Norway. It is even suggested it may date back as far as the Egyptians and Romans.

Whatever the origin, the combination of a tasty bread, scrambled eggs and smoked salmon produces one of the finest starts to the day.

## What you need

### For the Kneippbrød (Makes 2 loaves)

480 g coarse wheat flour
480 g white whole wheat flour
2 tsp salt
1 pack dry yeast
60 g butter
470 ml milk
235 ml water
½ tsp sugar
olive oil
butter

### For the topping (for 2 people)

6 eggs
30 g butter
2 slices smoked salmon
salt and pepper to taste
dill to garnish

## What to do

### For the Kneippbrød

Mix the flour and salt together in a large bowl. Set aside.

In a large pan, heat half of the milk with half of the water until warm. Ideally, use a thermometer and heat to 41°-46°C.

Add the sugar and stir. Slowly add the yeast to the warm mixture. Stir very gently with the end of a spoon to make sure the yeast is well combined. Set aside in a warm place until the mixture doubles in size.

Meanwhile, heat the remaining milk and water together in a small pan. Add the butter to the warm liquid until just melted, making sure not to boil.

Once the yeast liquid has doubled in size, alternate adding the yeast mixture and the water and butter mixture, to the flour a little at a time, stirring continually until a dough is formed.

Sprinkle flour onto a work surface. Place the dough on the surface and knead for at least 10 minutes. The dough should slowly spring back into shape when prodded.

Oil the inside of a large bowl with the olive oil. Place the kneaded dough in the bowl and cover with a damp tea towel or cloth. Place in a warm place until it doubles in size (1-2 hours).

Once risen, return the dough to the floured surface. Knead for another 5 minutes.

Divide the dough into 2 equal sized pieces and place each one in a lightly buttered loaf tin. Let the dough rise again for another 1-2 hours.

# 67 - Scrambled eggs and smoked salmon on Kneippbrød- Norway

When the dough has risen to twice the original size, place the tins on the lowest rack of an oven, preheated to 200°C.
Bake for 45 minutes and then remove from the oven to cool on a wire rack.

### For the topping

Place one slice of smoked salmon onto a slice of the Kneippbrød and set aside.
Heat the butter in a pan until just melted. Crack the eggs into the pan and stir immediately. As the egg starts to cook, stir to break it up into clumps of partially cooked egg. Remove from the heat while the eggs appear to be still undercooked as they will continue cooking in the hot pan. Keep stirring until the eggs are soft and fluffy but not overcooked, they should appear glossy. Divide the cooked egg between the slices of bread and smoked salmon. Season to taste with salt and black pepper. Garnish with the dill.

# 68 - Clootie Dumpling - Scotland

The UK is often mistakenly called England, much to the annoyance of the natives of the other three countries, Scotland, Wales and Northern Ireland, which make up the United Kingdom. Each of the countries has its own traditional recipes, some being variations of each other, and some being completely different to the other regions.

Many of the recipes have come about as the result of the scarcity of fresh ingredients, particularly in the winter, when most crops cannot be grown and the high cost of ingredients until the industrial revolution made the carriage of goods far less expensive. This forced the British cooks to be creative when it came to plying their craft and not only will you find dishes which are unique to the country but also to a region, or even a town.

As the British spread through the world, they came into contact with many other cultures, bringing back recipes and ingredients from far-flung places. Some were adopted outright, whilst others would be adapted to suit British ingredients. More recently, fusion cuisine, a blend of elements of different culinary traditions, has become widespread throughout the UK.

The clootie dumpling in this recipe can trace its origins back at least 300 years. It takes its name from the fact it is cooked in a cloth, or cloot in the Scottish dialect. The pudding is traditionally served at Christmas but also finds its way onto the Scottish breakfast table at any time of the year. It can be served with custard, cream or, believe it or not, it can be fried (hence served at breakfast), or just eat it as it is.

## What you need

500 g all-purpose flour
200 g beef suet
250 g caster sugar
250 g raisins
250 g sultanas
1 tsp ground cinnamon*
1 tsp ground allspice
1 tsp ground ginger
¼ tsp freshly grated nutmeg
3 tsp baking powder
½ tsp salt
2 large eggs
1 Bramley apple, peeled and grated
3 tbs black treacle
100 ml whole milk
extra plain flour for dusting

* 3 tsp mixed spice can be used instead of the cinnamon, allspice, ginger and nutmeg.

Suitable cloth (cloot) for containing the pudding **(see Cook's tip)**.

## What to do

Fill a very large two-handled pan with water to around 5-8 cm from the top; there needs to be enough water to allow the dumpling to float. Bring to the boil.

Whilst the water is heating, combine the flour, beef suet, sugar, dried fruit, spices, baking powder and salt, in a large mixing bowl. In another bowl mix the eggs, milk and black treacle together with the grated apple. Now combine the contents of the two bowls together.

Dip the dumpling cloot into the boiling pot of water to soak for a few minutes. Wring out the excess water. Spread the cloot on a large work surface and generously dust with an even coat of plain flour right to the edges of the cloth. The wet cloot and flour combine to form a protective glue-like waterproof surface.

# 68 - Clootie Dumpling - Scotland

Empty the dumpling mixture on to the cloot and draw it up around it. Tie with string, leaving room for the pudding to expand. Wrap the string around twice, and tie tightly. Leave enough to tie to the pan handles.

Cover and keep on a low simmer for 4 hours. When the dumpling is ready, lift out of the pan using the string. Remove the cloot and transfer the dumpling to a baking tray. Dry the dumpling for 15-20 minutes, in an oven preheated to 180°C. When the cloot is first removed, there will be a white glutinous skin covering the surface of the dumpling. After being in the oven, the surface will be darker and have formed into a crust.

**Cook's tip:**

Make sure to use a good quality tea towel, with a flat, dense weave, or something similar. Old pillow-cases were often used by the Scottish housewife making her clootie dumpling.

# 69 - Colcannon - Ireland

There is evidence that even as far back as 5,000 years ago, crops such as barley and oats were being farmed, oxen-drawn ploughs were in use, and enclosures were established to contain livestock. Sometimes this livestock was kept purely for milk which was used with the grain to make porridge, but there were periods when the emphasis was keeping the animals for their meat and the grain to feed the livestock. Chickens were kept by individual households for their eggs and meat. Vegetables such as carrots, parsnips, celery, turnip, cabbage and onion, didn't make an appearance until around the 8th century.

The revolution in food came in the late 16th century, when the potato arrived from South America. The conditions in Ireland were ideal for potato growing and they could be stored to provide food over the winter. It turned out to be a blessing and a disaster.

The population expanded rapidly, reliant almost entirely on this crop not only to feed their own families, but in many cases to sell to pay rent to the landowner. The poor of the land had become reliant on one crop for food and income and that's when the disaster struck.

In 1845, the crop was devastated by a fungal disease known as potato blight, which renders the potatoes inedible. The primary source of food and income for millions of people had been wiped out in one go. Farmers could no longer pay their rents and were evicted, and they could no longer feed their families.

Yet there was no shortage of food in Ireland, just that the wealthy landowners, many of them English, preferred to export crops such as vegetables and grain rather than feed the starving, whom they did not see as any concern of theirs, and the English Government did little to help. More than one million people died of starvation or disease.

Colcannon is a very Irish dish in that it is a simple to make, has few ingredients, yet is tasty and nourishing.

## What you need

4 potatoes (around 1 kg), peeled and cut into large chunks
2 tbs salt
5-6 tbs unsalted butter
3 lightly packed cups* of chopped kale, cabbage, chard, or any other leafy green
3 spring onions (including the green part), finely chopped
salt to taste
butter for serving

* the difference in weight for the same volume of these ingredients makes a cup measure more suitable

## What to do

In a medium pan, cover the potatoes with cold water by at least 2.5 cm. Add the salt, and bring to a boil. Continue cooking until the potatoes can be pierced easily with a fork. Drain in a colander. Return the pan to the cooker over medium-high heat. Melt the butter in the pan and once hot, add the greens. Cook for 3-4 minutes, or until wilted.
Add the spring onions and cook for a further minute.
Add the milk or cream, mix well, then add the potatoes. Reduce the heat to medium.
Use a fork or potato masher to mash the potatoes, mixing well with the greens.
Add salt to taste and serve hot, with a knob of butter in the centre.

# 69 - Colcannon - Ireland

# 70 - Banoffee Pie - England

The history of this firm favourite dessert is probably shorter than you would imagine and more than likely you will think of it as an American dish. Now world-famous, this sweet, irresistible and calorie-laden tart began life in a restaurant in East Sussex, not far from Beachy Head, on the south coast of England.

Owner of the Hungry Monk Restaurant, Nigel Mackenzie, along with his chef, Ian Dowding, were trying to improve on a recipe from the United States, Blum's Coffee Toffee Pie. This recipe was notoriously unreliable, sometimes having the consistency of concrete and at other times not setting at all. Whilst trying various combinations, Mackenzie suggested using banana along with the caramel and from this the banoffi, banoffee or banoffie pie was born.

Sadly, The Hungry Monk closed its doors for the last time in 2012, and Nigel Mackenzie passed away in 2015. The legacy that Nigel, Ian and the Hungry Monk left behind will no doubt live on for many generations.

This recipe varies from the original in that it uses a biscuit base rather than pastry and the coffee has been replaced by chocolate.

## What you need

### For the base

75 g unsalted butter
200 g digestive biscuits

### For the caramel filling (see Cook's tips)

150 g light muscovado or soft brown sugar
150 g unsalted butter
1 can condensed milk
pinch sea salt flakes

### For the topping

2 ripe bananas
150 ml double or whipping cream
100 g bar milk chocolate, grated

## What to do

Make the biscuit base first. Crush the biscuits in a food bag with a rolling pin, or pulse in a food processor until fine. Melt the butter in a medium-sized pan. Add the crushed biscuits to the melted butter and combine until evenly coated. Pour the mixture into the centre of a 23 cm/9 in, loose-bottomed, greased tart tin **(* see Note).** Then press the mixture firmly over the base of the tin and up the sides. Transfer the base to the freezer to chill for about 30 minutes, until very firm. Take the set biscuit base out of the freezer, remove from the tin.

Once the base is ready, make the caramel by heating the brown sugar and butter together in a pan over a medium heat, until the butter melts and the sugar has dissolved. (The sugar will not combine well with the butter until the sugar begins to melt).

Stir in the condensed milk and the sea salt. Bring to the boil, then take the pan off the heat while still stirring.

Pour the caramel onto the biscuit base then transfer to the fridge and leave to cool completely.

When ready to serve, slice the bananas and layer them over the set caramel. Pour the cream into a large bowl, and whip until thickened but not stiff. Spoon the cream over the bananas and spread until even.

Grate the chocolate over the top of the pie.

# 70 - Banoffee Pie - England

**\*Note** This is a delicate operation. If the base breaks when removing, just put the ingredients back into a pan, reheat until the mixture is soft and try again. Don't prepare the caramel until you have successfully removed the base from the tin unless you intend to leave in the tin for serving.
(After greasing the tin, I still found the base broke when removing. Adding food wrap to the inside of the greased tin allowed for easier removal).

## Cook's tips:

Two alternative methods of making the caramel are available.
1. Place an UNOPENED can of condensed milk in cold water and simmer for around three hours.
(Keep the can covered with water at all times, otherwise there is a risk of it exploding!)
2. Use a pan that is suitable for using in the oven, start as above then once the water has come to the boil transfer to a preheated oven at 140°C and cook for the same time. This is a much safer method than above.
After three hours, remove from the water and allow to cool completely before opening.
(To save power, several cans can be made this way and stored for future use).
Ready-made caramel can also be purchased.

# 71 - Welsh Mountain Lamb-Wales

Welsh cuisine grew largely as a result of the relative isolation of the Welsh people from the rest of the British Isles. The Welsh working people needed to base their recipes primarily on the limited ingredients they could produce or afford.

Most of the landscape in Wales is mountainous, which lends itself particularly well to sheep farming. The Welsh have farmed this way for many centuries and it is still practiced extensively today. Lamb and mutton are the meats most traditionally associated with the country and Welsh lamb is some of the best in the world.

Vegetables, other than cabbages and leeks - the leek is the national symbol of Wales - were rare. Leeks feature in a lot of Welsh recipes and can be used as an accompaniment to most dishes.

The humble potato took some time to be established and didn't really come into its own until the 18$^{th}$ century, despite having been introduced into the rest of Britain in the 16$^{th}$ century.

In the coastal and river regions, fish and shellfish dominated, much of the catch being wind dried and smoked, or preserved by salting. Salmon was so common that it was a staple diet for the poor.

## What you need

1.8 kg shoulder of Welsh mountain lamb (other lamb is acceptable)
1 clove garlic
125 g honey
450 ml apple juice, unsweetened
1 tbs apple cider vinegar
sea salt
freshly ground black pepper
1 tsp fresh mint, finely chopped
1½ tsp fresh thyme, finely chopped
25 g all-purpose flour
1 tsp lemon juice

## What to do

Rub the lamb all over with the garlic clove. Place the lamb on a piece of kitchen foil large enough to cover the joint with room to spare for the liquid. Place in a roasting tin.

Mix the honey, apple juice and apple cider vinegar then pour over the lamb. Season with salt and pepper then sprinkle the top with the mint and thyme.

Fold the foil over the top and place in an oven preheated to 230°C. Cook for 30 minutes. Open the foil and baste the lamb with the liquid, close the foil again and reduce the temperature to 180°C. Cook for a further 30 minutes. Open the foil and then cook for a final 40 minutes to brown.

Remove the lamb from the roasting tin onto a serving dish and keep hot.

Pour the juices from the foil into a saucepan. Leave to stand for 5 minutes then skim off any fat. To make the gravy, blend the flour with 4 tbs of the liquid then stir back into the saucepan. Bring to the boil, stirring continuously until smooth and thick. Season with salt and pepper to taste and add the lemon juice.

Serve hot with the lamb.

# 71 - Welsh Mountain Lamb-Wales

The lamb can be served with your choice of vegetables such as, baked onions, braised leeks, broccoli, carrots, buttered new potatoes, and of course, sprinkled with mint.

# 72 - Crème Caramel - France

Haute cuisine, most of us understand this to mean cooking of the highest standard, and it is no surprise that the term to describe such cooking, is French. In the middle ages, the French aristocracy often held banquets - the word banquet originally meant small bench. Not only was the food presented at these feasts cooked to the highest standard, but visual presentation was also highly prized. From this, haute cuisine was born.

Georges Auguste Escoffier is generally accepted to be the person who, in the late 19$^{th}$ century, modernized haute cuisine and made it what it is today.

He split the kitchen into five cooking stations or parties, which revolutionized the way dishes were prepared. The garde manger prepared cold dishes; the entremettier, starches and vegetables, the rôtisseur, roast, grilled and fried dishes; the saucier, sauces and soups; and the pâtissier, pastry and desserts.

A dish made up of several elements could now be prepared by multiple cooks, rather than one chef preparing it from beginning to end. This reduced overall preparation time and led to more complex dishes being attempted.

France and Spain both lay claim to this particular dish, but it is generally accepted to be French.

## What you need

### For the caramel

100 g sugar
4 tbs water

### For the custard

8 eggs
300 g caster sugar
900 ml milk
1 vanilla pod

## What to do

### For the caramel

#### Method 1:

Place the sugar and water in a small pan. Using a low heat, melt the sugar into the water then raise the heat to medium bringing the syrup to a boil. When it begins to turn golden brown, remove from the heat and pour into a large round casserole dish.

#### Method 2:

Place the sugar and water into the casserole dish and microwave on full power, initially for 1 minute, then in 20 second bursts until the syrup starts to change colour.

Both methods need a careful watch as it is easy to go from golden brown to dark brown and the caramel becomes bitter.

### For the custard

Lightly whisk together the eggs and sugar in a bowl. Pierce the vanilla pod in several places with the tip of a knife then place into a pan with the milk. Use a medium heat to bring to just short of the boil and then stir into the egg mixture (always add the milk to the egg mixture otherwise the eggs will cook in the milk and solidify).

Pour the mixture into the casserole dish.

# 72 - Crème Caramel - France

Place the casserole dish in a large pan (one suitable for using in an oven) and add sufficient water to the pan for it to come about two-thirds of the way up the side of the casserole dish.

Place in an oven preheated to 150°C and cook for an hour or until set. To test if the custard is cooked, use a bamboo skewer to pierce the custard, when it comes out clean, the custard is cooked. Allow to cool slightly then turn out onto a serving dish, sufficiently deep to take the caramel liquid. (Be bold when you turn it over or you will get covered in caramel).

Leave the casserole over the turned-out custard whilst it is cooling, to allow the last of the caramel to drip from the casserole.

Chill in a fridge before serving.

**Cook's tip:**

Vanilla pods can be dried out and used more than one time.

# 73 - Blueberry Pierogi - Poland

Pierogi were at one time considered to be a dish for the poor. During the 17$^{th}$ century, they came to be considered the staple food of Poland and gained popularity with the nobility as well as the peasants, so much so it is now considered to be the national dish of Poland.

Made from a basic dough, these dumplings are inexpensive and versatile; fillings can be savoury or sweet. A variety of shapes and fillings were adopted for special occasions.

Often, in English, you will see the plural of pierogi written as pierogis or pierogies, but in Polish, pierogi is the plural of pieróg, which is the generic term for dumpling.

Although this recipe is for blueberry pierogi, why not have a go making this with a variety of fillings? You know what they say, variety is the spice of life.

## What you need

### For the filling

165 g blueberries
2 tbs sugar
2 tsp all-purpose flour

### For the dough

225 g all-purpose flour
1 egg, beaten
pinch salt
60 ml milk

### To serve

Yoghurt
Sugar or honey

## What to do

### For the filling

Wash and dry the blueberries. Set aside. Mix the sugar and flour in a small bowl. Set aside.

### For the dough

In a medium bowl, mix the flour and salt. Make a well in the middle and crack the egg into the well. Mix the egg into the flour until evenly distributed. Add the milk and stir well. Add the water 1-2 tbs at a time, until a smooth and soft dough forms. Roll the dough out to about 3 mm thick. Add 2 litres of water, salt and little oil to a medium saucepan (the oil will help to stop the pierogi sticking together) Cover and bring to the boil.

Using a 9cm cookie cutter (or anything that is roughly 9 cm in diameter) cut the dough into circles. Re-roll the scraps until all the dough is used.

Place 1 tbs of berries on each round of dough. Sprinkle ¼ tsp of the sugar and flour mixture over the berries. Moisten the edge of each circle with a little water and fold the dough over the filling. Pinch the edges firmly to create a tight seal. When between 5-8 pierogi are filled and sealed, drop them into the boiling water. Boil until the dough is tender, 7-10 minutes. Use a large, slotted spoon, to remove the cooked pierogi from the water. Place on a plate. Continue cooking the remaining pierogi.

## To Serve

Mix the yogurt with the sugar or honey to taste. Serve the pierogi topped with the sweetened yogurt or use the yogurt as a dipping sauce.

# 73 - Blueberry Pierogi - Poland

**Cook's tip:**
Greek style yoghurt and honey are particularly good with this dish.

# 74 - Beef Short Ribs Sauerbraten - Germany

Mention German cuisine and most people will think of sausages, for which Germany is famous. This is understandable as there are over 1500 varieties available, but the cuisine is about far more than the humble sausage; many other ingredients are to be found in use in the German kitchen. Beef is not as popular as some of the other meats, but game meats such as venison and hare are widely available. Vegetables are used extensively in soups and stews, as well as an accompaniment to meat dishes. Freshwater fish are also popular.

Sauerbraten, meaning sour roast, was developed as a way of preparing the less tender cuts of meat, but is now used with other cuts because of its unique flavour.

## What you need

1.5 kg beef short ribs
salt and ground black pepper to taste
1 tbs vegetable oil
350 ml water
160 ml cider vinegar
160 ml red wine vinegar
12 juniper berries
9 whole cloves
2 bay leaves
1 tbs salt
½ tsp freshly ground black pepper
240 ml cold water
2 tbs butter
1 large onion, chopped
2 stalks celery, chopped
1 carrot, chopped
3 cloves garlic, minced
240 ml water
240 ml chicken broth
2 tbs white sugar, or to taste
120 g crushed gingersnaps
1 tbs balsamic vinegar
salt and pepper to taste

## What to do

Season the short ribs on both sides with salt and black pepper. Heat the oil in a heavy-bottomed frying pan over medium-high heat. Cook the short ribs, turning frequently, until browned on all sides, about 10 minutes (you will need to cook them in batches). Allow to cool slightly before transferring to a large bowl.

Pour 350 ml water, cider vinegar, and red wine vinegar into the warm frying pan and bring to a simmer. Cook and stir, scraping any browned bits off the bottom of the pan. Add the juniper berries, cloves, and bay leaves, salt and black pepper. Remove from heat and add 240 ml cold water. Pour the mixture over the ribs and place the bowl in an ice bath until chilled - around 40 minutes. Cover and marinate in the refrigerator for a minimum of 24 hours.

Melt butter in a large, heavy pan or Dutch oven over medium heat. Stir fry the onion, celery, and carrot in the melted butter until the vegetables are softened. Add the garlic and cook for a further minute. Place the marinated short ribs over the top of the onion mixture. Add 240 ml of water, chicken broth, and sugar to the marinade then pour over the top of the ribs.

# 74 - Beef Short Ribs Sauerbraten - Germany

Bring to a simmer over medium-high heat. Reduce to low, cover and simmer until meat is tender. Remove meat to a platter. Discard the juniper berries, cloves, and bay leaves - if you can find them! Sprinkle the cooked onion mixture over the top of the meat, reserving the excess cooking liquid in the pan.

Place the pan with remaining cooking liquid over medium-high heat. Use a food processor to grind gingersnaps until fine, then add to the liquid in the pan. Stir in the balsamic vinegar and boil until reduced and thickened; skim off any fat that rises. Season with salt to taste.

Strain through a fine mesh sieve, spoon over the beef, and serve.

# 75 - Langoš - Czech Republic

Lángos is a Hungarian national dish, but it is eaten in many homes and is widely served as a street food in the Czech Republic, where it is known as langoš (pronounced langosh). In the old days, the dish was made from bread dough. People would bake bread in the morning and would make Langoš to have for breakfast. The name derives from the Hungarian word 'láng' which means fire; every household used to have a stove, so langoš would be made over the fire. The Czechs and the Hungarians consider it to be the perfect dish, because it is filling and can be eaten with just about anything; garlic, cheese, sausage and a variety of sauces.

The Hungarians even made a song about langoš, which suggests that when the price of langoš goes up, the communist leader and regime will fall. Communism has fallen, but it was probably not related to the rising price of langoš.

This recipe was provided to me by Veronika Absolonová, a Czech citizen; you can't get more authentic than that.

## What you need

100 ml extra-virgin olive oil
2 cloves garlic, finely chopped
300 ml milk
½ tsp sugar
42 g yeast
500 g flour
½ tsp salt
oil for frying
150 g cheddar cheese, grated

## What to do

Add the garlic to the olive oil, mix well then set aside.
Mix the milk and sugar together then add yeast and let rest for 5 minutes. Sieve the flour and salt together into a mixing bowl then add the yeast mixture and make a dough.
Once the dough is mixed, leave at room temperature for 30 minutes.
Divide the dough into portions then roll them into flatbreads about 2 cm thick and leave for a further 10 minutes to rest.
Heat the oil in a large frying pan and fry the dough on both sides until golden brown.
To serve: brush with the garlic flavoured olive oil then top with grated cheese.
Can be served with a variety of toppings as you wish.

## 75 - Langoš - Czech Republic

# 76 - Borsch - Ukraine

Borsch, borshch, borsht, borscht, bortsch, if no one can agree on how to spell the name, what chance is there of agreeing on a recipe? That is certainly the case for this soup from Eastern Europe. The soup we know as borsch is Ukrainian in origin and is traditionally prepared using meat stock. The meat used to make the stock is added to the soup about 10-15 minutes from the end of the cooking time. However, every baba, or Grandmother, will have her own recipe, some with meat and some without.

The most commonly used vegetables used in borscht are beetroot, white cabbage, carrot, onion, parsnip, potato and tomatoes. Some recipes call for beans, such as red or white kidney beans, tart apples, turnip, celeriac, courgette and peppers. Tomato paste can be used as well as, or instead of, fresh tomatoes. Traditionally the vegetables are precooked - by sautéing, braising, boiling or baking - separately from the meat and only combined with the stock once cooked. This distinctive feature of borsch derives from the practice of slow cooking in traditional masonry stoves, which were used for both cooking and heating. This allowed the different cooking times of the ingredients to be taken into account, resulting in a dish that should be cooked to perfection.

This version contains no meat and is suitable for vegetarians.

**Please Note: This recipe produces over 6.5 litres of soup!**

## What you need

3 medium beets, thoroughly washed
3 medium potatoes, diced into bite-sized pieces
4 tbs vegetable oil
1 medium onion, finely chopped
2 carrots, grated
5 tbs tomato ketchup
½ head of cabbage, thinly shredded
1 can white kidney beans with their juice (red, if you prefer)
2 bay leaves
2.5 litres water
1.5 litres vegetable stock
6 tomatoes, peeled and pureed
4 tbs lemon juice
1 tbs cider vinegar
¼ tsp freshly ground pepper
1 tbs chopped dill
sour cream
dill for garnish

## What to do

Thoroughly wash the beetroot. Put the 2.5 litres of water in a large pan, then add the beets, ensuring there is enough water to cover. Bring to the boil then cover and simmer for about 45 minutes.
Meanwhile, put the 4 tbs of oil into a frying pan over a medium heat. Sauté the carrot and onion until they are soft. Stir in ketchup when they are almost finished cooking, then set aside.
Test the beets are cooked by piercing with a butter knife, which should slide easily into the beet. Remove from the water and set aside to cool. Reserve the water.
Add the diced potatoes to a large stockpot containing the reserved water. After 10 minutes, add the cabbage, carrots and onions and cook for further 10 minutes.
Once cool, peel and slice the beets into matchsticks then add to the pan along with
the vegetable stock, lemon juice, vinegar, pepper, bay leaves and kidney beans (with the juice). Cook until the cabbage is soft but still slightly crunchy. Season to taste with salt and pepper.

# 76 - Borsch - Ukraine

Serve with a dollop of sour cream in the centre and top with a sprig or two of dill.

# 77 - Bacalhau à Bras - Portugal

Like several European nations, Portugal once had a large empire and the influence on cuisine travelled in both directions. Brazil, Goa and Macau are some of the far-flung places where the Portuguese influenced the food, not to mention Africa, where corn was introduced as a crop by Portuguese settlers.

One contribution was so influential that in several languages throughout Europe, the Middle East and Asia, the product was named after Portugal. That product is the sweet orange, which the Portuguese brought from India and was a great contrast to the bitter oranges grown in Southern Europe at the time.

Japan first received refined sugar when traders introduced the Japanese to Portuguese confectionery, a delicacy revered by the Japanese aristocracy so much, that a Japanese variation of it was to become part of traditional Japanese cuisine.

Fish, particularly cod and sardines feature heavily in Portuguese cooking, unsurprisingly as the coastline of Portugal is entirely on the Atlantic Ocean. These are perhaps the two most likely foods that people will associate with the country, and it is one of these I have chosen to be a typical representative of the nation's cuisine. Cooked well it can be a delicacy, but be wary of badly prepared Bacalhau, as it may well put you of Portuguese food and that would be a shame as it has a so much to offer.

## What you need

400 g salt cod
500 g potatoes
1 large onion
2 garlic cloves
oil
6 eggs
pepper
parsley
salt to taste
black olives

## What to do

Soak the salt cod, for a minimum of two hours or preferably overnight, changing the water at least twice.
Remove the skin and de-bone, then break apart with your hands.
Cut the potatoes into matchsticks, the onion into fine rings and crush the garlic.
Fry the potatoes in a pan until cooked through and golden. Set aside to drain on kitchen paper.
In a deep pan, gently fry the onions and garlic until golden, then add the pieces of salt cod, and cook for a few more minutes, until the cod is just cooked.
Add the potatoes and stir whilst adding the lightly beaten eggs and pepper.
Stir for a few minutes, to create a scrambled egg mixture. Turn off the heat before the eggs solidify completely and continue stirring.
Serve hot, with parsley and black olives.

## Cook's tip:

Although the recipe suggests adding salt to taste, there is usually sufficient salt retained in the cod to avoid this being necessary. It cannot be stressed enough about the soaking of the fish as it will be salty and leathery if this is not done correctly.

# 77 - Bacalhau à Bras - Portugal

# 78 - Paella Marinara - Spain

Paella is perhaps one of the most popular and famous dishes of the world, yet it is almost impossible to define exactly what paella contains. There are as many variations of the dish as there are cooks, each claiming their recipe to be the best tasting or most authentic. Yet the dish originated from farmers and farm labourers cooking food over a wood fire, for their lunchtime meal. Valencia, the original home of Paella, has been one of the most important rice-producing areas in Spain since it was introduced by the Moors over 1200 years ago.

It is no surprise then that a cheap and simple meal would use rice at the main constituent, plus whatever else was available around the fields such as onions, tomatoes, snails, beans and perhaps rabbit or duck.

On special occasions, saffron would be added to produce a special colour and flavour, along with chicken.

Paella was traditionally eaten straight from the pan in which it was cooked, with each person using his own wooden spoon.

As 'Valencian rice' became more widely available, recipes were adapted with various types of seafood being added instead of, or as well as meat.

The traditional humble Paella Valenciana has no seafood but a mixture of chicken, rabbit and snails with green and white beans, but we are going to cook Paella Marinara.

P.S. if you don't already know, "paella" is pronounced "pa-e-ya" with the "e" as in "bet".

## What you need

25 threads of saffron, (a heaped ¼ tsp)
3 garlic cloves
1 sprig parsley
450 g boneless fish fillets, cod or halibut, cut into 5 cm pieces
salt and freshly ground black pepper, to taste
120 ml olive oil
8 langoustines or large whole shrimp
300 g cuttlefish or small squid, cleaned and cut into 2.5 cm pieces or rings
1 tsp smoked paprika (optional)
4 medium tomatoes, finely chopped
1 green pepper, cored and chopped
1 small onion, finely chopped
1.7 litres fish broth
500 g short-grain rice, preferably Valencia or Bomba (Arborio can be used)
200 g small clams, or mussels, cleaned

## What to do

Using a mortar and pestle, combine the saffron, garlic and parsley. Set aside.

Season fish with salt and pepper. Heat the oil in a 40 cm paella pan over medium-high heat then add the fish and langoustines. Cook until golden brown, turning occasionally (5-6 minutes). Transfer to a plate and set aside.

Add the cuttlefish or squid, paprika, tomatoes, garlic, peppers, and onions to the pan and cook, stirring frequently, until the onions are soft. Add the saffron mixture and broth, season with salt as required, and bring to a boil over high heat.

Distribute the rice evenly with a spoon and cook, without stirring, until rice has absorbed most of the liquid, (10-12 minutes).

# 78 - Paella Marinara - Spain

Reduce the heat to low, add the reserved fish and langoustines, press the clams or mussels, hinge side down into the rice. Cook, without stirring, until the clams or mussels have opened, the rice has absorbed the liquid and is al dente (any unopened clams or mussels should be discarded). Remove the pan from heat, cover with aluminium foil, and allow to rest for 5 minutes before serving.

This dish is best served at the table from the pan, allowing everyone to help themselves.

# 79 - Ravioli Foie Gras - Italy

Italy; the first foods we think about from this country are pasta, pizza and ice-cream, and it is one of these we will be cooking in this recipe. But there is far more to Italian cuisine than spaghetti, Margherita and tutti-frutti.

We can go back some 2,000 years to the time of the Romans, to see how important food is to the Italian culture, but it wasn't until the fall of the Roman Empire we started to see the diversity there is today. Once free of Roman rule, regional variations started to evolve, with specialisation appearing as some districts were more suited to cheese production, others to beef, etc. Influences from Greece and further afield soon followed, and as we have seen so many times throughout this journey, the cuisine became a melting pot of culinary methods and cultures but with the unique stamp of its home country.

## What you need (makes 48 ravioli)

240 g pasta flour (Tipo 00) **(see Cook's tips)**
3 fresh eggs
egg white
1 small jar of foie gras, or your choice of filling

## What to do

Sieve the flour into a bowl and make a well in the centre. Crack the eggs into the well then using your fingers, combine the eggs and the flour to form a smooth dough (this is when cooking gets up close and personal). If the dough is too wet, add a little more flour.

Once you have a smooth dough, the real work starts. To avoid heavy, stodgy, flabby pasta when cooked, gluten has to be formed in the dough, and the only way to create this (unless you have a bread maker), is to knead it. Roll it, stretch it, fold it, hit it, compress it, however you want to do it, but you have to work the dough until that gluten appears. It is hard work, that is why every Italian Grandmother has arms like a Russian shot putter. As you work the dough, you will notice it becoming more elastic, and this is what we are aiming for. Once this is achieved, separate the dough into equal size balls, wrap them all in a sheet of cling wrap to prevent them drying out and allow to rest in the fridge for 30 minutes.

**Whenever working on the pasta, keep all other pieces covered to prevent drying.**

### Pasta machine method

Flatten the ball with your hands then with the machine on the widest setting, roll the pasta through. Work through the machine setting getting a thinner sheet each time. Lightly dust both sides of the pasta with a little flour each time you run it through. Eventually you will have a long thin piece of pasta. When at the narrowest setting, fold the pasta in half lengthways, then in half again, then in half again once more until you've got a square piece of dough. Turn it 90 degrees and feed it through the machine at the widest setting, working your way through to the narrowest. Cover and work on the next ball of dough. Repeat for each ball until you have several sheets of pasta.

### Rolling pin method.

Very similar to above except you are doing all the work with a rolling pin. The sheet will not be square when you have finished, but with care when rolling there will be little wastage.

# 79 - Ravioli Foie Gras - Italy

**Making the ravioli**

### Ravioli maker method.

Lightly dust the frame with flour to prevent sticking.
Place a sheet of pasta on the frame then use the mould to create the pockets. Remove the mould and fill the pockets with the foie gras. Take care as the pockets are quite delicate. Brush around each pocket with the egg white then lay a second sheet of pasta over the first, pressing it lightly into the bottom sheet. Invert the frame on the work surface and carefully remove the frame from the pasta. Using a pasta cutter, separate into individual ravioli.

### Sheet method.

Lay a pasta sheet on the work surface. Place mounds of foie gras on the pasta sheet taking care to allow space between each mound. Brush one side of a second pasta sheet with the egg white, then lay over the first sheet, pressing down between the piles of foie gras. Use a pasta cutter to separate into individual ravioli.

Bring a pan of salted water to the boil then gently lower the ravioli into the water. Cook for 2-3 minutes until the pasta is al dente.
Serve immediately.

## Cook's tips:

Special flour is sold for pasta making. Normal flour can be used, but the pasta will not be as smooth as it would be using pasta flour.

You can choose pretty much anything for the filling. Cheese and meat are common ingredients. Various sauces such as cheese or tomato can be used, but for the foie gras it isn't necessary.
If you would like a sauce to go with it, there are recipes online for making foie gras butter. A little of this melted would be ideal.

Fresh pasta can be stored in the freezer for up to three months.

# 80 - Saganaki Garides - Greece

Greece is considered to be the cradle of Western Civilisation, and the birthplace of Western democracy, philosophy, mathematics, science and of course, the Olympic Games. These are just some of the things that the country has given not only to Western society but much of the world. The cuisine of Greece is very much along the lines of the rest of the Mediterranean, with olive oil, fish and lamb being prominent in the cooking. But it isn't just Western cuisine to be found in this country. Here we find dishes which would not be out of place on Middle Eastern and possibly Asian tables; baklava, gyros and dolmades spring to mind.

Saganaki gets its name from the two-handled heavy-bottomed frying pan in which it is cooked, the sagani. You may see saganaki referring to fried cheese, and that is indeed true, but not only for cheese. Anything cooked in the sagani is a saganaki; in this recipe, we are using shrimp or prawns which in Greek are garides, hence garides saganaki 'γαριδες σαγανακι.'

This dish is one of my personal favourites

## What you need

3 tbs olive oil
450 g medium size shrimp, peeled and deveined
4 cloves garlic minced
60 ml white grape juice
1 tsp white wine vinegar
1 large onion chopped
1 small chilli sliced
2 tsp chilli flakes
3 medium tomatoes, pureed or 1 can crushed tomatoes
120 g feta
salt and pepper to taste

## What to do

Preheat oven to 180°C

Heat 1 tbs of the olive oil in a frying pan on a medium-high heat. Add the shrimp and sauté for 4 minutes then add the garlic and sauté for a further minute. Add the grape juice and vinegar and sauté for 2-3 minutes. Set aside.

In another pan add the rest of the olive oil and sauté the onion until translucent. Add the chilli flakes and chilli and sauté for 2-3 more minutes. Add the tomatoes and simmer until the sauce thickens.

Pour the tomato sauce into the pan with the shrimp and mix gently. Place the mixture in a sagani or an oven proof casserole.

Crumble the feta over the top then bake for 15 minutes.

Garnish with chopped basil and serve with crusty bread.

## 80 - Saganaki Garides - Greece

# Conversion Tables

**Temperature**

| Temperature °C | Temperature °F | Gas Mark | Description |
|---|---|---|---|
| 110 | 225 | 1/4 | Very Slow |
| 120/130 | 250 | 1/2 | Very Slow |
| 140 | 275 | 1 | Slow |
| 150 | 300 | 2 | Slow |
| 160/170 | 325 | 3 | Moderate |
| 180 | 350 | 4 | Moderate |
| 190 | 375 | 5 | Moderately Hot |
| 200 | 400 | 6 | Moderately Hot |
| 220 | 425 | 7 | Hot |
| 230 | 450 | 8 | Hot |
| 240 | 475 | 9 | Very Hot |

**Dry Measure (US)**

| | |
|---|---|
| 1/16 teaspoon | Dash |
| 1/8 teaspoon | Pinch |
| 3 teaspoons | 1 tablespoon |
| 1/8 Cup | 2 tablespoons |
| 1/4 Cup | 4 tablespoons |
| 1/3 Cup | 5 tablespoon + 1 teaspoon |
| 1/2 Cup | 8 tablespoons |
| 3/4 Cup | 12 tablespoons |
| 1 Cup | 16 tablespoons |

**Liquid Measure (US)**

| | |
|---|---|
| 1/5 teaspoon | 1 ml |
| 1 teaspoon | 5 ml |
| 1 tablespoon | 15 ml |
| 1 fluid oz. | 30 ml |
| 1/5 cup | 50 ml |
| 1 cup | 240 ml |
| 2 cups (1 pint) | 470 ml |
| 4 cups (1 qt). | 950 ml |
| 1 gallon | 3.8 litres |

# Conversion Tables

**Liquid Measure (Imperial)**

| | |
|---|---|
| 1/4 tsp. | 1.23 ml. |
| 1/2 tsp. | 2.46 ml. |
| 3/4 tsp. | 3.69 ml. |
| 1 tsp. | 4.93 ml. |
| 1 tbsp. | 14.79 ml. |
| 1/4 cup | 59 ml. |
| 1/3 cup | 78 ml. |
| 1/2 cup | 118 ml. |
| 3/4 cup | 177 ml. |
| 1 cup | 237 ml. |

**Weight (Imperial)**

| | |
|---|---|
| 1 ounce | 28 grams |
| 2 ounces | 55 grams |
| 3 ounces | 85 grams |
| 4 ounces | 115 grams |
| 8 ounces | 225 grams |
| 16 ounces | 455 grams |

When measuring ingredients for cooking, it is important to ensure you retain the same measurement format throughout.

Whilst it isn't necessary to be too accurate with most measurements, there are some recipes such as those for bread, cakes, and meringues, where accurate measurement is essential. Any mistakes here will result in you producing something not quite as you intended.

It isn't possible to list all the conversion tables in a book such as this, as that would run to an entire book in itself, but there are plenty of websites that offer a range of conversion between the different measuring systems.

# Index

## A

**Apple**
  Apple Pie  128

**Aubergine**
  Berenjenas Rellenas 112

## B

**Banana**
  Banana and Date Mix 24
  Banana Pancakes 72
  Banoffee Pie 142
  Po'e 88

**Beef**
  Beef Rendang 70
  Beef Short Ribs Sauerbraten 150
  Bobotie 34
  Carne en Jocon 114
  Cazuela de Vac 90
  Curry Puffs 68
  Fajitas 122
  Mb'atten 12
  Papas Rellenas 102
  Pho Bo 64
  Salpicón de Res 108
  Silpacho 98
  Suya and Jelouf Rice 22
  Sweet and Sour Beef 80
  Thai Green Curry 58
  Veal Chops Green Peppercorn Sauce 36

**Beetroot**
  Borsch 154

**Blueberries**
  Blueberry Pierogi 148
  Fried Rabbit with Corn and Blueberry Salad 126

**Bread, Cake and Pastries**
  Banh Mi 66
  Black Bread 42
  Chimichurri Bread 92
  Clootie Dumpling 138
  El Postre Chaja 94
  Langoš 152
  Puff Puff 20
  Macadamia Nut Cookies 78
  Tequenos con Guasacaca 106

## C

**Cheese**
  Queso Fresco 110
  Sweet Potato and Pineapple Bake 82
  Tequenos con Guasacaca 106

**Chicken**
  Banh Mi 66
  Casado 110
  Chicken and Potatoes 10
  Chicken Yassa 16
  Kuku Wa Kupaka 26
  Sapa Sui 84
  Shandong Chicken 44
  Sichuan Stir-Fry 50
  Vori Vori de Pollo 96
  West African Peanut Stew 18

**Chillies**
  Ema Datshi 54

## D

**Dates**
  Banana and Date Mix 24
  Halawah 8

## E

**Eggs**
  Crème Caramel 146
  Huevos Rancheros 120
  Smoked Salmon & Scrambled Egg 136

## F

**Fish & Shellfish**
  Amok Trei 60
  Bacalhau à Bras 156
  Cangrejos Enchilados 118
  Fish Kabsa 4
  Fried Fish, Rice with Mushrooms 48
  Gumbo 124
  Paella 158
  Pescado a la Parilla Con Salsa de Mariscos 104
  Saganaki Garides 162
  Summer Casserole 132
  Tahitian Marinated Fresh Fish  86
  Tempura 46
  Tuna and Noodles 74
  Vatapá 100

# Index

## G
**Goat**
Ginger and Quince Stew 32
Goat Curry 116

## L
**Lamb**
Harira 14
Khuushuur 40
Kyrgyzstan Laghman 38
Kjotsupa 134
Mountain Lamb with Honey and Herbs 144
Mb'atten 12
Mutabbaq 6

## M
**Mango**
Mango Chutney 76

## N
**Nuts**
Macadamia Nut Cookies 78
West African Peanut Soup 18

## P
**Papaya**
Tam Som Salad 62

**Pasta**
Ravioli Fois Gras 160

**Peas**
Beya Kya 56

**Potato**
Aloo Dam 52
Bolo Polana 28
Chicken and Potato 10
Colcannon 140
Mb'atten 12
Papas Rellenas 102
Sweet Potato and Pineapple Bake 82
Venison with Sweet Potato Dauphinoise 130

## R
**Rabbit**
Fried Rabbit with Corn and Blueberry Salad 126

**Rice**
Fish Kabsa 4
Fried Rabbit with Corn and Blueberry Salad 126
Paella 158
Suya and Jelouf Rice 22

## V
**Veal**
Veal Chops in Green Peppercorn Sauce 36

**Venison**
Curried Gazelle 30
Venison with Sweet Potato Dauphinoise 130

Glen R. Stansfield is a qualified aircraft engineer, a profession he has pursued for over forty years. A lifelong interest in crime, in particular forensic psychology, led him to write his debut novel, *Fishing for Stones*, first published in 2015. His second novel, *Harry* followed in 2016.

He currently resides in Bahrain with his wife, Jess, and is an active member of the Bahrain Writers' Circle.

When not writing, he can sometimes be found on two wheels, often using his motorcycle to raise money for charity.

**www.glenrstansfield.com**

www.ingramcontent.com/pod-product-compliance
Lightning Source LLC
Chambersburg PA
CBHW042015090526
44587CB00027B/4265